DELIVERING THE GOODS

Delivering the goods

Education as cargo in Papua New Guinea

COLIN SWATRIDGE

Manchester University Press

Copyright © Colin Swatridge 1985

Published by
Manchester University Press
Oxford Road, Manchester M13 9PL

and 51 Washington Street, Dover
New Hampshire 03820, USA

British Library cataloguing in publication data
Swatridge, Colin
Delivering the goods: education as cargo in Papua New Guinea.
1. Educational sociology——Papua New Guinea——History
I. Title
370.19'3'09953   LC191.8.P/

Library of Congress cataloging in publication data
Swatridge, Colin
Delivering the goods.
Bibliography: p. 154.
Includes index.
1. Education——Papua New Guinea——Aims and objectives
——Case studies. 2. Consumption (Economics)——Papua New
Guinea——Case studies. 3. Cargo movement——Case studies.
4. Cults——Papua New Guinea——Case studies. 5. Papua
New Guinea——Social conditions. I. Title.
LA2270.P3S94   1985   370'.995'3   85-13761

ISBN 0 7190 1778 5 *cased*

Printed and bound in Great Britain by
Biddles Ltd, Guildford and King's Lynn

Contents

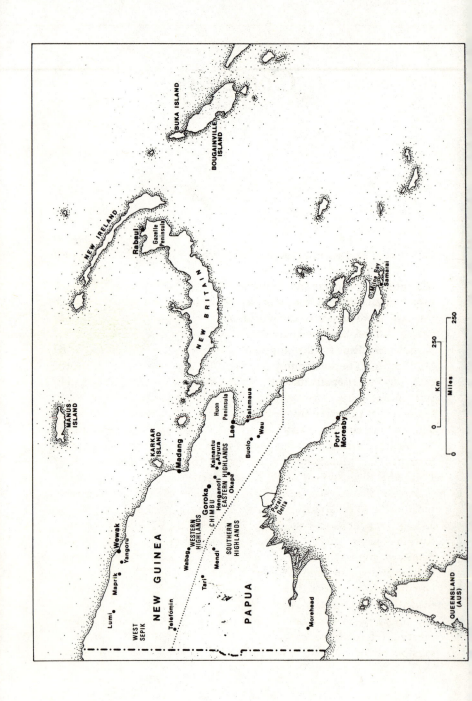

Introduction

Papua New Guinea is a long way away from the United States and Europe. It is a country about which Americans and Europeans have had little knowledge, and for which they have had still less responsibility. It has meant warriors in grass skirts, with bones through their noses; it has meant masks in a museum case, and exotic stamps, and very little else. It has meant much more to Australians, one hundred miles across the Torres Strait. The Southern half of present day mainland PNG (the former Territory of Papua) was placed under Australian control in 1905, after just twenty-one years of British rule. The northern half, German New Guinea, was occupied by Australian forces in the First World War, and was mandated to Australia by the League of Nations in 1920. So Australia's responsibility for its northern neighbour is of quite long standing; and such is the level of Australian aid to independent PNG, that the responsibility is still being discharged to this day.

Since independence, in 1975, Papua New Guinea has come to mean more to hundreds of young British and Canadian volunteers; and, as its education system has expanded, many British contract teachers have taught alongside Australian colleagues in the country's high schools. I myself taught English at two schools (junior and senior high schools) in the Eastern Highlands, in the late nineteen-seventies. Before I went, I read all that I could find to read about the country: articles in popular magazines, travel books, and books of an academic kind. I did not have to read far before meeting references to 'cargo cults'. These, I learned, are a modern version of the popular belief in the return of the dead, bringing

wealth and freedom, that is to be found in the religious movements
of many agrarian (or formerly agrarian) peoples of North America,
Africa, and Indonesia. Among the coastal tribes of Melanesia, this
belief found expression in the Oceanic Cult of the Ship of the
Dead.[1] Ghosts are white in Melanesia, as they are elsewhere,
therefore when white men landed in Papua (and) New Guinea they
were taken for ghosts. They brought unimagined riches with them,
but they did not bring freedom. For this reason, there has been a
conflict at the heart of 'cargoism': there has been the natural
struggle against invaders who have outlawed all that was most
exciting in the native culture; and there has been the natural envy of
Western goods that seemed to make life so much more worth
living. I read that the native peoples of PNG were disappointed in
their hopes of the cargo: it was made clear to them that it would not
come to them; they must make a road to the cargo for themselves
(what in Pidgin came to be called a 'rot bilong kago'). At one time
it looked as if baptised membership of the Christian Church was
the road; then, that it was an understanding of the Bible. It
occurred to me that western education might have looked like a
road to the cargo, and I wondered whether by going as a teacher,
earning a sizeable return from an investment in education, I would
not be promising goods that I could not deliver.

I continued to read on the job, and all that I read added to my
suspicion that schooling was understood in decidedly 'cargo' terms
– that fluency and literacy in English, especially, were sought after
for the access that they gave to jobs, and Toyotas, and houses of
man-made materials. The schools I taught in were boarding
schools, and my students came from far-flung villages whose
primary schools were less than one generation old. I asked my
students in Grades 8 and 10 (aged, at least, fourteen and sixteen,
respectively) to interview their parents: to have them recall their
hopes and expectations of the first schools in the villages; and to
record responses in written English. In addition, I interviewed
many of the same students willing and able to describe the activities
of local cargo cults, known to them either at first or second hand.
As I read, and as I interviewed, I became convinced that formal
schooling was a means to a material end, or it was nothing. If I was
surprised by this attitude, I should not have been; I had taught
English to boys in the south of Tunisia many years before whose

sole motive for learning it was to be able to sell carpets to English-speaking tourists; and I had been a student of comparative education for some years. Papua New Guinea means different things to different people, but there is a sense in which it has a meaning for all of us. It is a country of peculiarities, but there is much about it that commends it as a case-study of the development process the Third World over. I wrote down the responses of my student interviewees, I annotated what I read, and I made a case-study, with the object of writing as comprehensive an account as possible (within limited compass) of the reception given to formal education by people to whom the white men and all their works came as a quite considerable culture shock. I shall argue that the world view, the theology, the relationships in and between families and tribes, the economic norms and the notion of what constitutes knowledge among (some at least of) the peoples of Papua New Guinea, set the tone of their expectations of the outcomes of education. Furthermore, I shall argue that missionaries, government administrators, and educators themselves did much (unwittingly) to raise hopes and confirm suppositions that schooling would deliver the sort of goods that might be unloaded on the airstrip or the wharf.

To write this account, it has been necessary to apply to other than what might be considered to be the 'standard works' on the subject by informed outsiders. In addition to interview data, I have drawn upon travel and mission literature; on popular journalism; on research reports; on fiction; on biography and autobiography; on government publications; and on books about education and society in PNG, scholarly and otherwise. Because I wished to set this case-study of accelerated development, in the context of the more leisurely development process experienced elsewhere, I have included a few apposite quotations from the works of native African and Caribbean writers. Many more could have been referred to; but enough have been included to demonstrate that what has happened in PNG has happened (perhaps less colourfully) in other developing countries.

I had also to refer to works by anthropologists. The comic-serious joke was already old in the late 1970s that defined the extended family in PNG as consisting of mother, father, two or more children, paternal uncle, two or three cousins, and one anthropologist. Though this is not a book about anthropology for anthropologists, it is necessary to understand something of the cultural bed in which western institutions came to be sown. In the remainder of this introduction I shall confine myself to brief reference to what Meggitt has called 'the pervasive materialism of the people';[2] to sympathetic magic; and to the Messianic myth of Manup and Kilibob.

A good many writers have agreed with Meggitt: Read, for example, refers to the Gahuku people of the Eastern Highlands as 'materialists', who 'lose interest quickly in ideas and measure the good life in terms of worldly success'.[3] Harding and Lawrence,[4] likewise refer to the materialistic social values of the New Guinean for whom 'possessions are a pre-requisite of social relationships'. Payments abounded. There is an impressive unison of agreement among observers of a wise scattering of peoples that the Melanesian did not expect something for nothing, in this world or the next. 'Compensation' is a word that runs right through the literature, like a name through seaside rock. Marriage was (and is) an institution involving a lifelong series of payments throughout Melanesia. A man was never so weighed in the balance as when he was a bridegroom, and a woman was never so prized by her kin as when they set a bride-price on her head. This price was a payment made by the groom to the parents of the bride, and to her clan, as compensation for the loss of her services.[5] The husband was bound to compensate his wife in the event of a miscarriage, and for any injury done to her whether on purpose or by accident.[6] The husband in his turn was compensated by his wife's affines for her infidelity, among the Melpa people,[7] and for her desertion among the Chimbu.[8] Fatherhood, too, was told in pigs and pearlshells: when a child was weaned the father made payment to his wife's kin for the mother's milk that had nurtured it; when a child survived its first haircut – a proto-initiation – the father paid.[9] He paid because not to pay was to risk antagonising his in-laws, living and dead. And it was not only marriage that incurred 'compensation' payments: slander, theft, injury, and death in battle, were all occasions for material redress. If a step was worth dancing, if a story was worth telling, if an invocation was worth making – then it was worth paying for. Malinowski says of magic among the Trobriand Islanders that when spells were passed down from father

to son, there was no payment involved;[10] but when it passed out of
the nuclear family, to a younger brother or maternal nephew,
payment was in order, 'and (says Malinowski) a very considerable
payment it had to be'.

To give was to invest. To give a kinsman a thousand dogs' teeth
to help him keep up his bride-price payments was to impose an
obligation on him to make a return, in pots or pigs, in due season.
No one forgot such obligations; giving and receiving alike were
carried out in public. Giving was what justified ownership. The
wealthy man, the man with status in the tribe, was not the man
who hoarded – pigs did not live long, pork lasted no more than a
day or two, taro once harvested had a shelf-life of one week, and
sago starch was inedible within a month – the 'big man' was the
man who had so much to give that he could put his clan in his debt,
yet who gave only as much as the clan could repay. If he gave
more, he laid himself open to envy, and the fruits of ill will.
Dealings with other men were conditioned by the fact that those
men would one day be spirits. Their power for good or ill was yet
stronger in death than in life. Thus, when Lawrence speaks of the
religion of the Madang area as 'a mundane technology rather than
an other-wordly religion',[11] he means that it was the way in which
men (supposed that they) might influence the spirits of the dead in
the interests of the living. Beliefs and relationships were subject to
the rules of arithmetic: marriage was contracted, spirits were
respected, taboos were observed, prestations were made – all with
an eye to an access of material power (Pidgin 'paua'). Alternatively,
it could be got by magic, and the magic most often resorted to was
what has come to be called 'sympathetic magic'. McGregor lists it
among 'basic Papua New Guinea assumptions', that the 'power to
obtain material things and alter events may be secured through
physical association and imitation of those who already have such
power'.[12] This assumption explains much of the mimicry of
European activity that has always characterised the cargo cults.

The religion of the Melanesian Islanders was, strictly speaking,
henotheistic: that is, they appeased many gods, but gave credence
to one creator-god above all. Lawrence testifies to belief in Anut,
and his two sons Manup and Kilibob, among the peoples of the
Madang district.[13] Burridge witnesses to variants of the primal
myth among the Manam Islanders, the Tangu, and many other

peoples of the north coast of New Guinea.[14] And Strelan speaks of the myth of the two brothers as one of the most widespread motifs in Melanesian mythology.[15] Manup was the little piggy that stayed at home. Kilibob sought his fortune and found it, but he did not keep it for himself; he returned to Manup, and shared his riches with him as it befits a brother to do. Kilibob came to be the eponym of the white man, the Messianic man of invention, the man from across the sea, returned from the dead with freedom and wealth – with a new religion, with a magic book, with a language that all white men seemed to speak, with schools that would lead to jobs, and Toyotas, and houses of man-made materials – in a word, with 'cargo'.

Much was expected of the white man; and education was the hook on which most of these expectations were hung – indeed, schooling has been called the 'biggest cargo cult of them all'. Ivan Illich has damned schooling and cargoism in these words: '(Schooling) is a liturgical expression of a world-wide cargo cult, reminiscent of the cults which swept Melanesia in the 1940s, which injected cultists with the belief that if they put on a black tie over their naked torsos, Jesus would arrive in a steamer bearing an ice-box, a pair of trousers, and sewing-machine for each believer.'[16]

There was (and is) much about cargoism that is absurd, and that invited the mirth of cultured outsiders. But there was also much about it that was quite rational and hard-headed. There was a certain resistance to the discount of the old ways; but there was swift recognition of the practical significance of the goods the white men brought. It was obvious that the white man himself set a high premium on these goods; who was the black man to differ?

REFERENCES   [1]Lanternari (1965), p. 186.
[2]Meggitt, M. J., 'Introduction' in Glasse & Meggitt (1969), p. 3.
[3]Read (1966), p. 60.
[4]Harding, T. G. & Lawrence, P., 'Cash crops or cargo?' in Epstein *et al.* (1971), p. 168.   [5]Strathern (1972), p. 125.
[6]Ryan, D'Arcy, 'Marriage in Mendi' in Glasse & Meggitt (1969), p. 3.
[7]Strathern, Andrew & Marilyn, 'Marriage in Melpa' in *ibid.*, p. 144.
[8]Brown, Paula, 'Marriage in Chimbu' in *ibid.*, p. 94.
[9]Strathern (1972), p. 2.   [10]Malinowski (1974), p. 226.
[11]Lawrence, P., 'Daughter of time' in Harding & Wallace (1970), p. 271.
[12]McGregor (1976), p. 189.   [13]Lawrence (1964), p. 21.
[14]Burridge (1969), p. 64.   [15]Strelan (1977), pp. 60, 61.
[16]Illich, Ivan, *De-Schooling Society* (Penguin Books, 1976), p. 50.

1

Contacts
and converts

It was gold that first attracted white men up into the Highlands in any numbers. Government patrols climbed into the Upper Ramu Valley in 1926 and 1929; and the Rev. W. Bergmann established a Lutheran Mission station in what is now the Eastern Highlands, at Kambaidam.[1] But it was a gold prospector, Ned Rowlands, who began a systematic penetration of the region, in 1928; it was in response to Rowlands' first reports of gold-finds that a party of twenty-five miners left the less than easy pickings at Edie Creek to try their luck in the mountains. This was in April 1930, and the leader of the expedition was Michael J. Leahy. It had been supposed that the Highlands were barren: that there were few if any people living on the edges of dense woodlands, and wastes of crag and scree. It was only when men could take in square miles of land at a time, from the cockpit of a Junkers W34 or a Fox Moth, that it could be seen how wrong this supposition was. The prospectors could be irritated by prying eyes, and excited, jostling bodies, preoccupied as they were by the search for gold;[2] but it was only from the air that Mick Leahy fully understood just how many small, stockaded villages there were. A small plane could land on a strip it need take no more than a few hours to clear. And so Europeans had their first sight of stocky, warring Highlanders; and the Highlanders had their first sight of Europeans, in the person of Mick Leahy, Major Harrison and Ian Grabowsky, pilot and giant.

Grabowsky has been described as one of the tallest men in New Guinea.[3] He stepped out of the Moth at Bena, in March 1933, wearing a white flying-suit, a white helmet and square, green goggles, and stood head and chest above the 'Kanakas' who came to see what manner of bird it was that had landed among them. Mick Leahy wrote later that they 'simply flattened into the ground and moaned'.[4] It was the common lot of the first Europeans to enter the Highlands to be taken for returned ancestors.

It is a happy circumstance (for researchers of all kinds) that, since this first contact was made within still-living memory, in the late twenties and early thirties,[5] there are still men about who were there, with sons and grandsons at school who can pass the story on. One of my students, Asada Umoro, described the scene (orally) thus:

> When the first Europeans were coming, the village people killed pigs and prepared food for them; and they were wondering what kind of people they would see. Suddenly, they arrived, and some of the Europeans seemed to the people as though they were their dead relatives. They treated them kindly, and some village elders tried to see how they ate food, cooked, slept, etc.; and they tried to imitate them, but they couldn't do it.

The white man wore such curious clothes: shoes, gloves; he carried equipment from another world. At a stroke, he made fire; at a few more strokes, he felled trees that it took Highlanders days of patient worrying with axes of sharpened stone to fell.

Jim Taylor, assistant district officer based at Salamaua, was another big man. He walked into the Upper Ramu in June 1932.[6] He tells the story of his contact with natives near Kainantu, in the Annual Report of 1933–4:

> Generally we were received well and without hostility. Weapons were seldom seen, and we were regarded in awe as something ghostly or supernatural. In some parts we were regarded as people returned from the dead; some of the party were actively recognized as ones who had died in recent years . . . The recognized ones were asked to stay and take their old place in the community . . . When I removed my hat they would gasp 'Oh!' and talk excitedly, and hold their children up to get a good look at us. In other places they appeared awe-stricken and dazed.[7]

If fear was the first of the Highlanders' feelings on seeing white men, other feelings followed soon after. Paulias Matane,[8] in his children's story *Aimbe The Challenger*, describes the first landing of an aircraft on an upcountry airstrip: 'As soon as we were at the side of the airstrip, we heard the great noise of the plane a long way away. We stretched our necks and strained our eyes. Soon, over the hill, we saw a small speck. Some thought it was a bird, but it gradually became bigger as it came closer. When it was near, we ran for our lives into the trees.' From behind the trees, the natives heard the bang and rattle of bags and packages being thrown from the plane out on the grass. Fear then quickly turned to curiosity: 'As soon as the plane had gone, we raced down to the airstrip (and) excitedly collected the cargo.'

The aeroplanes that had opened up the Wau–Bulolo gold fields – that had, in fact, airlifted the town of Bulolo piece by piece from one airstrip to another – were light biplanes, even Junkers G/31s, the most advanced aircraft in the world. But from 1929 onwards they began to lose their novelty value. In 1931, aircraft in Stone Age Papua New Guinea carried almost as much cargo as all the aircraft in Britain, France and Germany together. And by the mid 'thirties, more cargo was being carried by air in Papua New Guinea than the total air cargo carried in the rest of the world. The Highlander, perforce, became accustomed to the sight and sound of aircraft. Davies mentions that planes had only been landing in Wabag (Western Highlands) for a few years before the 'wild people' of those parts were mounting on the aircraft to refuel it, or to bring out the cargo, 'with the same nonchalance as if they were working on a farm cart'.[9] If, as Rowley says,[10] technology was being revealed to the villager in reverse, and he was seeing his first aeroplane before his first wheelbarrow, the experience was not too disorienting for too long.

But the first sight of a European had by most Highlanders was of an Australian foot-patrol, flanked by armed native policemen, and followed by a line of carriers, bearing food, camping equipment, bedding, medical supplies, and a radio, the wonder of wonders. And if they were not government officers in khaki drill, they were Lutheran missionaries, in black and white, with Bibles.

A student, Ika Tira, describes the scene in his village at the coming of the first missionary:

> It was a sunny day when the people from my village went together to catch rats to make my uncle into a young man, when he was going to be known as a man. Women, girls, and small children were at home cooking and preparing food for the celebration. When the men were

hunting for rats they saw the first missionaries come off the bush road. Some of the men ran away, but brave men stood back and wanted to spear them. They threw spears but they missed them.

Then one of the missionaries put his hands up and did actions not to kill them. Some of the men would not listen to him, or whatever sign was made they would not hear.

Just then, one man stopped them from thowing spears and told the other villagers that he was going to talk with the missionaries, but he said: 'If they attack me, all you must rush in and kill them'. When he went close to them, they didn't do anything but showed him a Bible book and made good to him.

There was cause for apprehensiveness on both sides. White men could as well be taken for evil spirits as for benign ancestors. Another student, Humime Fameso, tells the conventional tale of cannibals and cooking-pots: 'Most of the people thought these Europeans were the evil spirits from somewhere. The acting patrol officers who came to the village were killed and were eaten by the village people in the Highlands.' When this happened, retribution was swift and terrible. The New Guinean had nothing to teach the European about 'payback'.

The returning ancestor, white as befitted a spirit, was so embedded in native mythology, that for every Highlander who ran away from the first Europeans in terrified disbelief, two others approached them cautiously, as if to ask: 'What took you so long?'.[11] It was the 'cargo' that the Europeans brought with them that really broke down native defences. Brown observes that 'Chimbu feelings towards the Europeans were fear mixed with desire for the white man's goods'.[12] The experience of the three Leahy brothers (Mick, James and Daniel) bears out this observation. They were the first white men to make contact with tribes in the central and western Highlands, up above what is now the Daulo Pass, west of Goroka. When the tribesmen first saw the flashlights and axes, the ciné camera, the radiogram, and all the other marvels that the expedition possessed, they gaped and kept their distance. Daniel Leahy takes up the story:[13] 'The first time they were curious and frightened. The second time they said: "we're not going to let the treasure pass out of our hands a second time". They wanted the axes. We had to let them see we were armed. We had good weapons. We made it clear: "We'll do the same to you. You leave our stuff alone, and we'll leave your stuff alone".'

In time, the 'Kanakas' could do more than covet some at least of the gods of the white men. Cheap blankets, hurricane lamps, canned food, cigarettes and cotton clothing could all be bought at the trade store. Young men came home with these things from the plantations on the coast, and old men could not for long maintain a pretence of scorn. Cargo was dropped from aircraft, or unloaded from ships at wharves, and all that white men had to do to take possession of it was to make marks on a piece of paper. No white man seemed to dig, or heave, or carve, or carry. He sat, sweating at a table, and made signs on paper that his God-above-Sydney read, and heeded. This was the marvel of them all, that reading and writing and issuing orders in a strange language was all the 'work' that a white man ever seemed to do.

Daniel Leahy is an honest man. He does not disguise his motive, and that of other prospectors like him, for pushing on up into the Wahgi Valley, the heartland of the Westland Highlands: 'We all had the gold fever. El Dorado was always at the end of our trip. It is no good saying we weren't old colonials. We were. We weren't up there for a sun tan. It's no good saying I went up there for the good of the natives, because I didn't. I went up there for the sake of Mick and James Leahy. And I didn't do too badly out of it.' Planters 'didn't do too badly out of it' either. The Leahys discovered this about the 'natives' that 'for one shell, they'd do about a month's work' panning for gold; planters had already discovered that a few silver shillings, and rather less than full board, bought the services of climbing-boys for the three or four years of a very binding contract. The natives had no use for surplus coconuts and they had no use for the silver shillings that those coconuts could earn. Villagers had no natural urge to be 'useful' to the white man, so the white man resorted either to the stick or the carrot. In Southern Rhodesia, as Lawrence Vambe tells us,[14] white settlers resorted to the stick: 'The Europeans were angered not only by the supposed sloth and primitive state of evolution of the Shona, but perhaps more so because the black people of Mashonaland showed a defiant indifference to the religions of money and fortune-making which had brought the settlers this far . . . However, the Europeans, having the power to enforce their will, decided on coercion.'

The planters of New Guinea more often resorted to carrots. All that it was necessary to do to make their shillings 'useful' to the

workers on the plantation was to make trade store goods available
of a sort that (a rather large number of) the shillings would buy.
The promise of matches, blankets, suitcases and axes was enough
to lure and retain hundreds of young men in compounds many
miles from home. One can believe that white settlers were sincere
in their belief that 'contact with the white man will inevitably
hasten the (black man) along the path that leads to civilization;[15]
one can agree with Tomkins and Hughes that many of the men
who came into the lives of the natives were 'dedicated people
whose intent was to help and teach the native people, to bring them
the benefits of learning and civilisation'.[16] But one can also heed the
caveat entered by Willis when he observes of the planter's vision
according to which the labourers returned to their villages 'to act as
a civilising leaven amongst their brethren', that this was nothing
more than a rationalisation for the German need for cheap labour.[17]
There was not only one sort of planter, any more than there was
only one sort of gold prospector, missionary, or government patrol
officer – or, for that matter, one sort of New Guinean villager. The
white men who took off, or set sail for New Guinea, were a mixed
bunch; one would expect them to have had mixed motives for
going. And so they did.

If parents sold their sons to the planters' recruiting agents for no
more than a bush knife and a few beads (as Burridge claims),[18] it
need not be assumed that the contract was not satisfactory to both
sides. It is only now, when the citizens of independent PNG reflect
upon how much they gave away for so little, that they complain
that they were duped. Then, a bush knife, or steel axe, was the
difference between the work of days and the work of hours. And
the young men would return to them with money to buy labour-
saving devices in plenty. In the event, it was not long before the
young men saw that their hard-earned shillings would not go very
far. Even when they had bought their blankets, their cotton shirts,
and a cardboard suitcase to put them in, their position in relation to
the white man had not changed at all.[19] They would earn a few
shillings and the European would keep many more for himself;
they would spend their few shillings and have nothing left and the
European would spend many times more shillings, and still his
purse would be full to overflowing. The white man not only made
the good things to buy, he also made the money with which to buy

them.[20] It might not have been the white man's intention to make his black labourers dependent upon him, it might not have been his ambition to play the 'masta' to black slaves, but this was often what the relationship amounted to. A certain sort of German planter had very little to learn from planters south of the Mason–Dixon Line – or south of the Zambezi, for that matter. It was fortunate for the master in this context, that the New Guineans were less obviously jealous of their personal freedom than the Shona, in Vambe's Southern Rhodesia:[21] 'The concept of hired labour was completely unknown to my people, and this innovation cut right across the most sensitive areas of what the Shona understood by personal freedom. It was bad enough that the Europeans were taking their land. But by demanding their labour as well they were stripping the Shona of the last vestiges of the little freedom that they still possessed.'

The concept of hired labour was unfamiliar to the New Guinean, too, but he did not resist the innovation. On the other hand, he paid a high price for his access to the 'modern sector' and his growing dependence upon it. Cash was free from old obligations; and yet cash in turn imposed its own obligations on the earner, and the spender. They were not as obvious to the native as the old ones, but they were no less unrelenting. They could resemble the obligations of the addict to his drug. European money was spent in the (often) Chinese-run trade store. The Chinese were especially active, as 'pushers', is Epstein's Rabaul,[22] and Willis's Lae,[23] both towns on the Northern New Guinea coast. Willis in particular speaks of the natives of the Huon Peninsula as increasingly dependent on the European goods and foods that they could buy in the Chinese trade stores. He names 'metal cooking utensils, knives and axes, matches, lamps, garments, mirrors, soap, paints, tea, bread, sugar, rice and tinned meat' as the articles most often stocked and sought after.[24] Not only did the stores play an important part (as Willis says) in 'westernizing the villages' about Lae; there was no stopping the migration of some of the novelties up into the most accessible of the Highland villages. It was contrary to local norms for an individual to accumulate wealth, yet the Highlander craved the trade store goods of the white man that only the hard-working individual could earn. Since that individual was often a young man far from his village, he only really came into conflict with village norms when he returned home. The villagers themselves envied him his possessions, and shared them in some measure, yet they were powerless to acquire them. They badly wanted the ends, but they could not work the means.

But there was another sort of cargo than the sort that could be bought. The first white men made promises for which their audiences would hold them to account. Matane puts the following words into the mouth of 'an elderly, self-confident District Commissioner':[25] 'There will be big things coming to your once isolated area. More roads will have to be built, and I have a man right here who is responsible for road building . . . Some schools will be opened here so that your children can go to school and learn about the things that we white people know.' This was a promise indeed. At first (as a number of my students testified) it was believed that, by going to school, children would learn the language of their dead relatives. Thus, Samiro Manopi reports: 'When the missionaries started the mission school in my area, they thought that this was to teach their language and ways to communicate with dead relatives, especially white people.'

The teachers themselves, Josiah Sore says, were thought to be the villagers' ancestors, 'who died a long time ago, were sorry for them, and came back to life to help their children and them'. A third student (Alo Kukari) takes this thought a stage further: 'When the school came the people thought that they (the teachers) were going to educate their children, and go back to the dead relatives' place, and bring all the good things by the help of their children who were being educated.' The white man's goods had a 'mystical source'.[26] They came into being by magic. Reference has been made to the strong indigenous belief in sympathetic magic, or the transmission of magical power by close association. As hopefuls had clustered about big men, waiting for power (Pidgin *paua*) to rub off on them, so now they associated with white men in the same expectation. It might be enough to have a trade store in the village: money would pass backwards and forwards, and magic-ally, profits would flow. But it was better by far to have a living, breathing white man on hand. Young men in their teens and twenties could work for white men on the plantations; they could watch them and imitate them, dress like them and pick up Pidgin. But for older men there was no alternative to having a white man come to them in their village. Read tells of Makis,[27] a man of thirty six, who applied to the local patrol officer (or 'kiap') for a white man to live in his Gahuku village in the Eastern Highlands. Read himself was this 'white man'. He recalls how he searched for the motives of this Makis in asking for a white man: 'I concluded that he expected to obtain from me the kinds of benefits that were provided by European planters in the area . . .'.

If they could not have a white man, they could at least have his proxy. The black boys who went to work for Europeans, or – better still – went to their mission schools, could be the mediators of the white man's wisdom. The sympathetic magic was attenuated at this remove, but it was better than nothing.

'Houseboys' were in a strong position to learn the secret of white power. Matane's Aimbe was the servant of the itinerant Mr Manki.[28] Having touched Mr Manki's 'strange things', Aimbe was 'kept awake most nights thinking that he must have a much stronger magic than ours'. He thought to himself: 'I want the good magic from Mr Manki, but how can I get it? . . . By staying close to him, I may pick up some of his secrets . . .'. When white visitors mislaid one or another of their possessions, the likelihood was that it had been appropriated, not for its own sake, but for the sake of the magic that it was thought to command. Daniel Leahy was himself the victim of petty theft in this cause: as he stood among tribesmen (he recalls), 'I felt hairs being pulled from the backs of my legs – and they were being wrapped in a banana leaf'.

In his short story 'Tax', John Kadiba has a young man return to his village,[29] and his admiring relatives:

> 'I work in a white man's house,' said Koro with confidence.
> 'And all these ant eggs (rice), this cane, this sago and this smoke, did you buy all these?'
> 'Buy them? No, aunt. Do you think white people have to go far to look for food? They don't work for it. All is ready at their hands. There's a special place where all the food is kept . . . Food just comes. They write what they want on bits of paper and send them away. The food just comes.'

As with food, so with axes, blankets, paraffin lamps and all else that the white man had and the black man wanted. His religion and magic had not brought him any of the items of hardware that he so craved, and the traditional ceremonies weren't delivering these goods now that he could ask for them by name.

The obvious recourse was to a new magic and a cult informed by observation of European practice. This was not always 'religious' practice, since patrol officers often made earlier contact with (and did more to pacify) the New Guinea Highlanders than even pioneers among missionaries. A student (Wayawani Kavare) writes about cult activity in his village (in the Okapa sub-district of the Eastern Highlands) following the visit of patrol officers in 1954 – a very late date indeed:

> When the first white men came to my area they brought 'foreigners' from other parts of PNG. They brought kina and toea shells and said they'd brought them from the beach, to trade with them for food. The villagers had had these shells before but they hadn't known where they'd come from. They supposed the shells had come from the stones (they didn't know what a beach was). They built houses and decorated them with leaves and made flower gardens around them. They went out to the rivers and collected stones to become shells. Important people, big men, were responsible for positioning the houses. Women and children were not allowed to see what was going on, or approach the new houses. The reason was they thought the women and children were weak, and the magic might be powerful enough to kill them.
> When they brought the stones from the river, they rubbed them with leaves and vines before placing them in the houses. My father and step-father were among those chosen to stay in the houses during the hoped-for transformation. They had been doing it for a couple of years before they gave up hope and burned down the buildings.

Though this is a late account, it is consistent with accounts of earlier cult activities of a 'non-Christian' kind. Strelan,[30] a theologian, speaks of these 'cargo cults' as having existed long before the arrival of the gospel. They were not a mere mimicry of European forms, he says. And Opeba agrees:[31] the cults were 'clearly indigenous in nature, and revivalistic in that they tried to renew the old social order based on the traditional principles of life'.

One of the first cults that clearly was influenced by Christianity was what bemused expatriates called the 'Vailala Madness'. Though this took place in Papua (in the Gulf District) it was a type to which later movements, elsewhere, conformed quite closely. It erupted in 1919, in response to a sermon preached by a white missionary, on the resurrection. Attention was paid to the symbolism and ritual of the church and administration, in that tables were set up for feasting, decorated with croton flowers in beer bottles: stealing and adultery were to be forsworn, and Sunday was to be observed; 'Djaman' (German) was what the movement's leaders claimed to be talking in their frequent bouts of glossolalia; and Evara, the founder of the movement, wore European clothes. We learn this much from the account of the 'Madness', by an anthropologist Peter Worsley.[32] But there has been doubt and disagreement about what meaning the cult activities had for those who listened to Evara's prophecies of the coming of the cargo. They believed in his steamer in a quite literal sense, there is no doubt about that; but did they reject the old rituals, or resurrect them? Did they court the missions, or revile them? Did they want Europeans to stay, or did they want to drive them out? And was the pole, with its cane string hanging from the top, an imitation telephone, as F. E. Williams (government anthropologist of the day) said it was; or was it 'an analogy of the recently erected radio masts not for away', as Rowley claims;[33] or was it nothing of this imitation sort, but a representation of the sacred tree of *Melare*? This is Albert Kiki's explanation.[34] The so-called Vailala Madness was not a cargo cult at all; 'cargo may have come into it,' he concedes, 'but the main purpose of all this strange behaviour was an attempt to contact the dead'. Kiki was 'caught up in the madness' as a boy; now as a respected indigenous writer, and elder statement, he can admit that the cult leaders entertained 'the most absurd notions'.

Many meanings have been inferred from the cargo cults. Lawrence regards the early cults as an attempt to reinterpret, and re-inspire the Manup-Kilibob myth.[35] The Lutheran Turner looks upon them as the expression of a deep longing for fullness and humanity and for equality with, and acceptance by, whites and other peoples of the world.[36] 'European interpretations of the cults agree that they rooted in the deep need of the native peoples to explain, to their own satisfaction, how it was that the white men had so much and were so powerful, and how they themselves had so little and were so weak. What Vambe says of the young men of Mashonaland,[37] holds good for the more thoughtful young men of New Guinea:

Men of his age group, while gladly coming to terms with the materialism of white civilization, were both angry and confused. The reason was that they could not reconcile their way of thinking with that of the tribal system whose inglorious past, inadequate present and uncertain future held few attractions for them. Neither could they find psychological satisfaction in the Church whose mysticism, compromising position, obsession against wealth and ill-defined moral strictures were not related to their youthful dreams.

The dreams of a youthful New Guinean had been of fighting, and winning. Fighting had been the *raison d'être* of most able-bodied males before contact, therefore, they needed to understand why their battle prowess had been set at nought by so few. If their own religion had been a 'mundane technology', they needed to know what manner of engineering it was that had secured such good fortune for the white man. Burridge's Tangu people observed that the white man was immune against sorcery, yet he concerned himself with spirits of a kind, called 'jems' (germs) against which he took all sorts of precautions.[38] His pharmocopoeia seemed so much more impressive to the Tangu than their own 'meagre techniques for countering sorcerers'. Beliefs and practices, masks and initiations, superstitions and men's houses, dances and taboos were being called into question by men who said 'do this' and it was done.

The villager had grown up to believe in the swift and merciless justice of the raiding party; in the natural enmity between neighbouring clans; in war spoils and compensation. Non-affines were foreigners, and foreigners were fair game. If they possessed more than you did, it was because they had stolen it from your forefathers by fighting or by sorcery. It was but a short step from gazing at the white man's goods, to seizing them in 'retribution'. According to the myth, Kilibob would share his fortune with Manup. The day would come when Manup would lose confidence in his brother's good intentions towards him, and cease to be satisfied to gaze on Kilibob's goods. For the time being, however, he was content to gaze on his god.

There is some evidence for the view that in New Guinea, the old religion was ceasing to satisfy, and that Christianity offered an escape from onerous taboos and obligations – even fear. It was an idea whose time had come.

The soil was not uniformly fertile at all altitudes; but it was fertile in Lae, Willis tells us,[39] because the religion of the local Kawa people was particularly burdensome to them, imposing on them, as it did, all manner of 'interwoven religious and social duties'. Such a system, he says, contained 'many of the seeds of its own destruction'. The white man had brought Christianity, and the symbols of new knowledge – woven cloth, books, pottery, matches and steel axes. He had brought his language with him, and writing – marvels that he seemed quite prepared to teach. The white man's language was at its most marvellous in the Bible that each one carried with him. The Austrian explorer, prospector and man of parts Wilhelm Dammköhler was taken for a missionary by villagers on the Morehead River, in 1898. Not wishing to disappoint them, Dammköhler did his best to act the part: 'The chief signed to me to read prayers (he said later), whereupon I opened my Byron and read some stanzas out of that . . . I remained with these friendly natives a fortnight, mixing freely with them . . . and kept up my missionary character all the time, reading to them out of my Byron morning and evening during my stay'.[40]

Christianity was associated with literacy from the first. Books were the strongboxes of the new knowledge that only the white man's learning would unlock. There were those who thought they could buy this learning: McGregor speaks of illiterates from distant villages making the arduous journey to Lumi (in the West Sepik) to purchase Pidgin songbooks.[41] Certain of the missionaries themselves were by no means scholars, but villagers' demands made teachers of them all the same. He who read and wrote was flattered into teaching the unlettered to read and write. It was part of the doctrinal equipment of the Lutheran and the evangelical missionary that the Bible should be made known to all men. Villagers were no less enthusiastic about education than the missionaries; indeed (White suggests)[42] they may even have been more so. The latter taught converts to read and write – in a vernacular or lingua franca – so that they could read the Bible in their own villages or be trained as pastors and catechists, to evangelise further afield. Literacy was the means to a confessional end (just as it was in the early Victorian Sunday School), it was not the end itself.

This is neither to be wondered at nor deplored. Yet, inasmuch as the missions enjoyed a virtual monopoly of education, the new knowledge was bound to be thought of as religious knowledge. Education was literacy, was Bible-reading, was Christianity, was civilised values, was education. The equation was offered, and accepted. The missionaries chose to teach literacy in one or other of the native languages because in this way, villagers would take hold of the message and pass it on. This is why it was so important to teach able converts with a knowledge of Pidgin or Motu (in Papua), who could act as intermediaries and apostles for the cause. The civil authorities in Papua preferred the missions to teach in English, in the long-term interests of administrative efficiency and social control. Sir William McGregor noted with satisfaction in 1899 that the London Missionary Society was leading the way in conducting several of their schools exclusively in English.[43] Oram, however, reports that only the brighter children in the Port Moresby district were taught in English; and Lawes confirms that Motu was adopted as the lingua franca in the LMS schools of his day.[44] The natives themselves might well have been undecided one way or the other (knowing no better) in the early days of the mission schools; but as missionaries fell under the suspicion of keeping their secrets in English, and as English speaking school leavers jumped the queue for jobs, so (says Willis) the English language took its place in the lengthening equation of perceived goods.[45] Furthermore, the city was given the beginnings of its edge over the village. If English was taught in town it paid to billet children there, on complaisant relations, so that they could learn the real thing.

Those boys enjoyed a special advantage in village society, and urban employment, who served an apprenticeship as mission boys. Fear had inspired natives to confer special privileges on white missionaries: a grade ten student, Alo Kukari, put it thus: 'The missionaries lived in separate houses and village leaders told the people and children not to enter the houses, because if they did, then the spirit of their dead relatives will disappear and they will never see them again. Every time when the ladies came back from gardens, one of the persons from each family had to bring food to the missionaries. They didn't have to go close but stayed some yards away.' The villagers built these separate houses, and a building to serve as the church. They dug and planted the mission gardens, and gave freely of the fruits of their own. The missionary and his wife may have accepted these goods and services as no less than their due – they in their turn looked after the sick, attended to sores, and dressed the wounds and bruises of the battle-field. Villagers who got more than they gave wondered when they would receive the bill, since – as one chief in the Western Highlands put it to the Catholic W. A. Ross[46] – 'in our way of life, nothing is given for nothing, and we presume you are the same'. 'What do you want from us?' the chief asked; 'when is the pay-off?' Ross had waited six months for this question, so his answer was ready: 'We do not want your land, your women, or your pigs (he said). We wish to open a boarding school where your boys from the age of ten to sixteen will be taught to read and write. You have seen us looking at books, writing on paper. This art we shall teach your boys; they will live at our mission station and go to school each day.'

Ross was a more patient pastor than most, or perhaps by the time missionaries had reached the Highlands they had shed the old paternalism of the coast. For there is abundant testimony to cases of intimidation on the part of both Catholic and Lutheran missionaries. Lawrence, for example, claims they 'exhorted and abused people, and threatened them with punishment from the administration if they failed to send their children to school'.[47] Clarke speaks of more subtle bribery,[48] and of the mission's preference for boarding over day schools: at boarding schools, the boys would be beyond the powers of the village to undermine the church's teaching. The philosophy of the Jesuit College lived on. The effect of this policy and practice was to drive a sizeable wedge between the generations: boarding school boys were detribalized; even boys who lived at the mission within sight and sound of their family's huts enjoyed certain of the privileges of their white patrons. All were spoiled for life on the land, for subsistence farming and simplicity. Their attention was turned to the airstrips, and the buildings of permanent materials, and the jobs in offices and shops. They became, in White's words, 'apprentice white men'.[49] Like the young plantation labourers, they had money, they had status, they had Pidgin and they had an interest in change. When church dues and taxes were introduced in 1920, the church gave a significant fillip to monetisation and to the still greater glory of those able to pay. But nothing so whetted the appetite for consumer goods as the sight of them in white men's houses. Worsley speaks of the contradiction noted by natives, between 'mission teaching and the lives led by the white men he met'.[50] But it has to be said that these white men included the missionaries themselves. They said: 'Thou shalt not covet'; and they preached Galilean simplicity. Yet the missions were themselves a source of European goods.[51] The missionary wore clothes of woven stuff, ate out of packets and sat at table. He may not have been rich in any absolute sense, but it was vain for him to vilify riches. He had access to riches; he had enjoyed them; he knew their secret. Benjamin Umba writes thus in a recent novella:[52] 'The permanent residents at Denglagu were (sic) the missionary, a middle-aged, energetic and ambitious man whose land was flowing with cars, nice clothes, steel buildings and good food, all of which simply 'appeared' to his people. There was little work in it. This was the land of the white man.'

The missionary might have renounced these things; he might now denounce them; but he could not help representing them. Cars, of course, came later. Western technology did not have to be so far above the heads of the natives to inspire awe and covetousness. The more primitive technology of steel axes, razor-blades, matches and pencils was impressive enough – and no missionary did without these, or would have considered doing so. The two cultures were so distinct that the simplest artefacts could excite possessiveness. The pagan religion had stood sponsor to what there had always been of material things; so the juxtaposition of Christianity and western technology argued the same strong relationship between the two novelties. It is not surprising that baptism was interpreted as an initiation into a European 'package deal'. Conversion was supposed (because it was said) to ensure spiritual rewards; and what conversion had begun, prayer would sustain. The cargoist Mambu lost patience with the missionaries among the Tangu: he accused them of deluding the people, and of keeping the cargo secret to themselves. He did not revert to paganism in his disgust; instead, he built a 'church', he administered 'baptism' to his followers and said his prayers in the mission-taught manner.[53]

The missionaries set unfortunate examples, and sowed unknowing confusion, in other ways. Conversions did not come easily at first, therefore, just as certain pastors offered bribes to children to attend school, so others made conversion and baptism worthwhile for the few individuals ready to take the plunge.[54] Guiart points out that in photographs in the abundant missionary literature of the time, native converts are shown black and beaming in presents of pristine white laplaps, alongside the clergyman in tropical kit, and his good lady.[55] The bestowing of such gifts, of course, set a precedent that could not be followed for long. Thus, as new converts were made in expectation of similar 'spiritual rewards', gifts were of a humbler order, or wanting altogether. What were the natives to make of all this? The missionaries made it plain that they sought to make converts; they made a few, after months, even years, of patient labour, and they rewarded them. Then, when all their prayers seemed to be answered, and conversions could be numbered in three figures, the flow of rewards dried up. Were the mass baptisms not a cause of congratulation; and did not the missionaries boast of their success to the bishop, to the kiaps and to the mothers' unions back home? Confusion was sown and the plant was disillusionment.

Furthermore, missionaries, who preached against tribal fighting and village factionalism, were not above a little striving themselves. Each denomination (except the Catholics and the Seventh-Day Adventists) agreed to be confined to a zone, or zones of influence. It was not difficult for a few denominations to co-operate in the early days when there were few sowers, and limitless good ground: fiefdoms in Papua went uncontested right up to 1930.[56] But it became impossible to preserve the old boundaries as the number of denominations grew, and Catholics and Seventh-Day Adventists refused to be confined. Rowley counted thirty four missions representing eighteen different Christian churches, in 1964 – in New Guinea alone;[57] in Papua, eleven denominations maintained a further seventeen missions. The Methodist Threlfall writes: 'It was naturally confusing to the people to see two groups of Christian missionaries who did not work together and whose ways of worship were so different.' The churches' attitude towards paganism and cargoism, however, was still more suggestive. The missionary was in a cleft stick. His own devotional language was full of the vocabulary of sin and paganism, antichrist and spirit possession, Satan and the Powers of darkness. It came naturally to him to regard his native charges as heathens destined to wail and gnash their teeth. The question was whether it was more merciful to be tolerant and permissive, or zealous and no-nonsense. Such a proclamation as that of the Evangelical Lutheran Church of New Guinea, in 1964, dignified cultism in a quite unintended way. The statement included these words: 'These things are nothing but illusions and deceptions of Satan . . . Sometimes a person says . . . that in a dream he received a prophetic message or that he communicated with a spirit. This is a trick of Satan himself.'[59] Such inflammatory talk could rebound on the church when, for one reason or another, the natives rejected its teaching; then Satan could sound like an attractive alternative to a God who had proved less than generous. Missionaries who purported to 'cast out devils',[60] or who (if they were Catholics) sprinkled holy water on them,[61] could not at the same time deny their existence. Indeed the more casting out and sprinkling they did, and the more they forbade dancing and flute-playing, the more credence they gave to the spirits they affected to mock.

Not only was the time right for the new religion, the old religion was itself a soft landing-place for Christianity, particularly when this was of the apocalyptic sort. The lack of a long time-line in what there was of a native sense of history lent startling immediacy to the Christian story. Jesus might have died a mere dozen wet seasons ago, and he might return at any time at all. Strelan has identified five themes common in the old Melanesian paganism: the division of mankind; the conflict between two brothers; the lost paradise; the coming of the end-time; and the intervention of a saviour-hero.[62] A religion containing these themes could digest the stories of the Tower of Babel, the murder of Abel, the expulsion of Adam and Eve from Eden, the Revelation of St John and the Incarnation, without much difficulty. Tribal banquets prefigured the Last Supper; prayer, prophecy, messianism and ritual cleanliness had all played a part in the old religion, therefore they were acceptable in the new. The fact that natives had been conditioned to observe a hundred and one taboos every day of the week explains their preference for the Old Testament (with all its familiar 'Thou Shalt Nots') over the New Testament; and the otherwise unaccountable success of the Seventh-Day Adventist Mission. This mission was particularly strong in the Kainantu sub-district, where a student, Mainia Ta'e wrote thus:

My father said the first education came to the village was brought by the native SDA mission. These people were the first people to go to my area. They went and made friends with the people. There they built a temporary education house with bush materials. In that house they called in boys and girls and they taught them how to speak Pidgin, weave walls for the house, sing songs, and taught them to bath three times a day. Beside these things this SDA mission made strong rules, like having a day off on Saturday, telling people not to work in the gardens or do any other thing. They also told them not to eat pigs. It was some sort of belief against their mission.

Not to eat pork was an especially heavy cross to bear; but what was pork to be weighed in the balance with life in the Kingdom? A religion that promised rewards in an after life, and a general resurrection of the dead, was a religion that villagers could understand and respond to. They could respond to millenarian imagery; they could respond to balletic ritual; to the opportunities for the enhancement of status offered by church offices and council membership; and they could respond to formularies said, or sung – especially sung. Singing had worked magic in the old religion; now, the powerful voices of Fijian, Samoan, and English missionaries promised a yet more powerful magic whose benefits villagers were keen to secure, so they sang as lustily as they knew how. There was no knowing to what goods this delightful duty might lead.[63] And if singing worked in church, there was no reason why it should not work in school. 'Five days a week the children strained their lungs and vocal cords singing their alphabets and numerals. The teachers did not seem to be bothered by the noise. The parents heard their children's voices when they passed by on their way to the garden. To them it was evidence that their children were learning – though it seemed to have little significance for them what their children were learning'.[64]

And here was the rub for the more thinking European churchmen. The response of the villagers to the outward forms of the new religion was keen and quick. It was audible and visible, and gratifying. But there was no knowing how deeply the inner meanings were understood. Old Testament stories were evidently enjoyed: God took the cargo away from Adam because he had had sexual intercourse with Eve; he took the cargo away from Ham because he had mocked his father's nakedness, so he was transported, like a convict, to live on bare necessities in New

Guinea, and father tribes of the dispossessed.[65] It hardly mattered that Old Testament stories were melted down to be re-cast in cargoist moulds; there was after all, much in the Old Testament that the sensitive westerner found unpalatable as it stood. But it did matter that a similarly literal, materialistic, interpretation was put upon the more spiriual events of the New Testament. It was a little disturbing that natives found the miracles so much more to their liking than the parables,[66] and that the Sermon on the Mount was set at such a discount. And on another plane, it was a cause for anxiety that congregations made so little of the meaning of the Crucifixion and Resurrection of Christ. McCarthy's story about the self-sacrifice of the Catholic and ex-mission helper, Loren, in Madang, is evidence of the potency of religious symbolism, and the limits of the understanding.[67]

Much of the blame for the misinterpretation of Christian teaching has to be laid at the door of translation. Biblical theology has much to do with language. Once the gospels and epistles had been rendered into English, interpretation achieved its own momentum for English speakers (just as Lutheran's translation had underpinned Lutheran hermeneutics for German speakers). Now that the New Testament stories were having to be translated into Pidgin, and into hitherto unscripted vernaculars, it ws obvious (even to Europeans who did not have a firm hold on native languages) that something was being lost.

As Lawrence puts it:[68] 'The limitations of (Pidgin) vocabulary glossed over petty idiosyncrasies and hence accentuated the essential oneness of meaning'. It might be counted for gain that the forced choice of simple terms negated centuries of scholastic cavilling at a penstroke. But when the only word for 'God' was one that served in the vernacular for spirits good and bad, the entire apparatus of Christian belief in an Omnipotent Father could hang upon the use of an alternative term. And more broadly, there was nothing that translations could do to prevent native-language speakers charging Matthew Chapter 7, verses 7 and 8, with full-blooded cargo meaning. To be told to 'Ask and it shall be given you; seek and you shall find . . . for everyone that asketh receiveth; and he that seeketh findeth' was what the villager wanted; it was why he had joined. He needed no instruction when it came to asking, or seeking; all he wanted to know was where to look. The imagery was remote – few natives had seen or would ever see a lamb, for example – and this made for real difficulties. But even when bread and wine could be seen and tasted, to try to present them as symbols of flesh and blood was to court misunderstanding. Missionaries and translators not only had to choose their words carefully, they had at times to re-think their message. Those that did not either never knew just how fundamental native misapprehensions could be, or they experienced too late what Rowley calls the shock of 'sudden revelations of the inadequacy of a lifetime's work'.[69]

The ambivalence of the natives themselves made life difficult for the conscientious clergyman. What was offered might be received whole-heartedly, or be flatly rejected. There was almost no telling beforehand what the response would be. This is not a cause for surprise when one considers how much the cultural novelties on offer must have taxed the native imagination. There must have been much heart-searching, for example, before parents would commit their sons to the mission schools. One student, Yowis, Irompe, quotes (and translates) his grandfather as saying: 'At that time when the schools were introduced to the people of my area they thought and wondered what the word school meant. When their children were taken to school, they thought that one day their children will be like the white man . . . Some even thought that they will become a big man after learning the new things.' Other parents (perhaps in the same village) had other ideas. Yanu Mo'a reports: 'When the schools were first introduced in my area, people did not respond very much. They ignored the school and objected to their children going to school, although their children very much wanted to go. The parents thought that their children would not return to them, once they had been taught the strange ways of the white man.'

The white man brought the Bible, and God, reading and writing, money, and singing, and technology, all on the same ship, or the same plane. The mission appeared to be at the intersection of all these roads to the cargo. It was an appearance that beguiled for a time – but only for a time. Of all the roads, literacy appeared to be the widest and straightest. After all, white men whose connection with the mission was tenuous at best – men at the patrol office and the plantation boss's house, at the Burns Philp warehouse and the airport terminal – these men all spoke and wrote English. They did not walk about with Bibles, and sing, and lay down the law about eating pork or playing the flute on Sundays, yet they had cargo enough to satisfy the most covetous of natives. Those who were perceptive as well as covetous, products of the mission schools perhaps, and of the plantations, learned to doubt whether Christian observance was the 'miraculous bridge' that would lead them to the wealth, the privilege and the power of the Europeans, that it had seemed to be. Read goes on: 'Left to the mission and its lay evangelists, the bridge would prove to be a chimera, for they offered only the bare rudiments of learning sufficient to string some semi-literate sentences together and to read with difficulty, a few sacred texts transcribed into a tongue no white man would bother to try to comprehend.'

Others – perhaps no less perceptive in their way – did not place all their confidence in Christianity, preferring instead to absorb what seemed good in the new dispensation, and to combine it with what had seemed good in the old. Subsistence farmers planted coffee bushes to please the white man, but their wives continued to grow sweet potatoes on forty-five degree slopes. Villagers sent their eldest boys to school, but they kept the young ones and the girls at home. The sick went to the mission or the aid post for European medicine when they suffered from a 'European disease', but they applied to the old remedies to exorcise spirits, when sickness was deemed to be the work of the sorcerer.[71] And the same eclecticism was evident in the religious domain. Feacham identified three kinds of 'convert': the enthusiast who underwent baptism and attended church regularly; the half-hearted who was baptised and who attended church for social or prudential reasons; and the unclubbable, who was persuaded of the existence of God, but who did not join in any of the activities of the mission.[72]

The villagers of Nzekwu's Nigeria found the missionaries and their sermons 'unattractive and boring'.[73] They learned to interpret the mission schools for what they often were: 'a cover under which Christianity would operate . . . the essential thing to (the missionaries) was not the teaching of reading, writing and arithmetic . . . but the spread of the foreign faith. As soon as the mission hospitals were built even those institutions became a means of spreading the faith.' Many, perhaps most, of those claimed for the faith by the missions held to a Christian belief shot through with animism. The most apparently committed of Christians might retain elements of a 'pre-Christian' world view. In one of Aluko's Nigerian novels, two educated Christians differ in shared doubt:[74] '"If you were a true Christian, Elder, you would not believe in ghosts." "Teacher, you are black, I am black. Don't let us lie to each other. Even Christianity cannot explain certain mysterious things in this country. Even the White Man's magic cannot explain these things. Teacher, there are ghosts".' And (black) Prime Minister Michael Somare confesses in his autobiography to 'personal experiences that I cannot explain by anything that I was taught in a white man's school'.[75]

The Summer Institute of Linguistics (SIL) is an American mission whose objectives are to devise scripts for unscripted languages, and to translate the Bible into as many of them as time and resources allow. The mission is a thriving community, with its own shops, post office, telephone exchange, airstrip and school, at Aiyura, in the Eastern Highlands. Those who live there are academics – mainly researchers in linguistics – and translators, and evangelists who spend months at a time out in the villages teaching and preaching. A student, Sion Akwanda, lends some credence to the view that there were missionaries who gave an unintended impetus to Christian cargoism. Sion refers to the belief prevalent among Kasoru villagers, in Okapa, that the SIL missionaries were ancestors returned from the dead. He writes:

> During 1965 and onwards, some of the linguists from SIl went there (Kasoru) to translate the language, and they needed these people who were following these cargo cults, but they didn't tell them that they were following the wrong way. They still tried to encourage them to carry on these cargo cult activities. And they even talked with language people and said 'brother' and 'sister', but these people didn't tell them that this was a wrong idea. They said this might be your brother or sister. They were interested in cargo cults.
>
> The language people even brought clothes to the villagers and told them that these were the clothes sent in by your friends or relatives. The linguists didn't tell the villagers that these cargo cults were not good, but they tried to put the Christianity and cargo cults together.

Better known examples of this sort of syncretism are afforded by the Paliau Movement on Manus, combining elements of the

Christian view of God, with the worship of ancestral spirits,[76] by the prophesyings of the West Papuan, Christian Angganita;[77] and by what Fergie has called the 'fascinating' and 'essentially very Christian' movement of the prophetess Philo, of the Mekeo people of Inawai'a.[78] Christian converts rejected traditional knowledge in favour of the new – but they did so conditionally. They accepted that you could not make money by praying, however earnestly, but (says Morauta) few Chritians could forswear money-making magic with perfect confidence.[79]

Schooling had the effect of increasing the distance between the domains of the old and new knowledge. Knowledge had conferred status in rural Melanesian society – particularly if it was knowledge of an arcane, spell-binding sort. Knowledge of the means by which wealth might be accumulated and disposed of to the maximum advantage was a prerequisite of leadership. As young men went to school, and grew away from the village; as they learned how the white man acquired wealth, investing time, effort, and capital, in profit-making enterprise, so the old knowledge suffered an irreversible loss of prestige. Young analysed the essays of school students in 1972, and again in 1975, for the expression of attitudes towards traditional and modern knowledge respectively.[80] His finding was that: 'Faith in modern knowledge is strong while traditional knowledge is stigmatized . . . Modern knowledge was held to be responsible for development and for an easier life for Papua New Guineans; traditional knowledge was held to be responsible for much fear, sorcery, and killings'. Inasmuch as the education system was highly selective, those who made it to the top of the pyramid were an élite few. The fact that these few had survived a long and arduous climb ensured that the new knowledge was regarded by those who had not survived, as still more esoteric than the old, and still more worthy of respect.

Many writers testify to the frankly instrumental acceptance of Christianity by villagers accustomed to thinking of spirits as beings whom it was possible – even necessary – to manipulate. 'Take the feeding of the 5000', says the missionary McGregor.[81] 'We need to take care that the Christian message is not presented in a way that will reinforce wrong assumptions'. In his still less optimistic moments, McGregor must have known that the natives were probably more interested in the wrong assumptions than in whatever the 'right' ones might have been. Graham Smith, a retired missionary in Mendi, reflects on early popular interest in the gospel:[82] 'When I went to new areas folk pleaded for someone to come and teach them about Jesus . . . This happened so often and the cries were so persistent that often I felt helpless that we couldn't respond to their requests. Now I realise, of course, there were mixed motives for such requests. The people knew that if the mission came a certain amount of economic activity would come.'

The same mixed motives lay behind the early, and late, enthusiasm for education, as Young's point above, about modern knowledge, makes clear: education was the road leading to development; and development led to an 'easier life for Papua New Guineans'. Pupils and their parents would put the same construction on going to school, as they had put on going to church. The teacher was no more likely to disabuse his clients of the misconstruction, than the missionary. As often as not, they were one and the same.

References

[1]Sinclair (1971), p. 2.
[2]ibid., pp. 9, 10.
[3]Souter (1963).
[4]ibid.
[5]Brown (1973), p. 3; Finney (1973), p. 19.
[6]Sinclair (1971), p. 19.
[7]Territory of New Guinea *Annual Report* 1933–4, pp. 115–17, in Jinks *et al.* (1973), p. 268.
[8]Matane (1974), p. 15.
[9]Davies (1970), p. 172.
[10]Rowley (1965), p. 27.
[11]Souter (1963), p. 234.
[12]Brown (1973), p. 66.
[13]In oral commentary for the film *First Contact* broadcast on BBC2, 3 February 1984.
[14]Vambe, Lawrence, *An Ill-Fated People*, London HEB (1972), p. 101.
[15]Australian newsreel commentary, in n. 13 above.
[16]Tomkins & Hughes (1969), p. 20.
[17]Willis (1974), p. 46.
[18]Burridge, K., 'Mambu' in Jinks *et al.* (1973), p. 194.
[19]McGregor (1976), p. 180.
[20]Eri (1973), p. 45.

[21]Vambe, op. cit., p. 99.

[22]Epstein (1969), *passim.*

[23]Willis (1974), *passim.*

[24]ibid., p. 112.

[25]Matane (1974), pp. 17, 18.

[26]Downs (1972), p. 15.

[27]Read (1966), p. 14.

[28]Matane (1974), p. 11.

[29]Kadiba, John 'Tax', in Beier (1972), pp. 21, 22.

[30]Strelan (1977), p. 11.

[31]Opeba, Willington, 'The Peroveta of Buna', in Trompf (1977), p. 213.

[32]Worsley (1970), pp. 93–6.

[33]Rowley (1965), p. 50.

[34]Kiki (1968), pp. 50, 51.

[35]Lawrence (1964), p. 93.

[36]Turner, H. W., 'Foreword', in Strelan (1977), p. 6.

[37]Vambe, op. cit., p. 12.

[38]Burridge (1960), p. 70.

[39]Willis (1974), p. 19.

[40]Souter (1963), p. 111.

[41]McGregor (1976), p. 190.

[42]White (1965), p. 120.

[43]McGregor, Sir William, 'British New Guinea' in Jinks *et al.* (1973), p. 65.

[44]Oram (1976), p. 16.

[45]Willis (1974), p. 146.

[46]Ross, W. A., 'The growth of Catholicism in the Western Highlands' in Jinks *et al.* (1973), pp. 272–3.

[47]Lawrence (1964), p. 83.

[48]Clarke (1975), p. 163.

[49]White (1965), p. 120.

[50]Worsley (1970), p. 49.

[51]Willis (1974), p. 36.

[52]Umba, Benjamin, 'The fires of dawn' in Greicus (1976), p. 19.

[53]Burridge (1969), p. 65.

[54]Worsley (1970), p. 218.

[55]Guiart, Jean, 'The millenarian aspect of conversion to Christianity in the South Pacific' in Harding and Wallace (1970), p. 401.

[56]Smith (1975), p. 13.

[57]Rowley (1965), p. 155.

[58]Threlfall (1975), p. 60.

[59]Strelan (1977), p.93.

[60]Rowley (1965), p. 143.

[61]Lawrence (1964), p. 79.

[62]Strelan (1977), pp. 60, 61.

[63]Threlfall (1975), p. 39.

[64]Eri (1973), p. 2.
[65]Lawrence (1964), p. 76.
[66]Hogbin (1951), p. 244.
[67]McCarthy (1963), p. 241.
[68]Lawrence (1964), p. 235.
[69]Rowley (1965), p. 149.
[70]Read (1966), p. 107.
[71]McGregor (1976), p. 185; see also Rowley (1965), p. 143.
[72]Feacham (1973), p. 40.
[73]Nzwkwu, Onuora, *Blade Among the Boys*, London HEB (1972), pp. 86, 87.
[74]Aluko, T. M., *One Man, One Wife*, London HEB (1967), p. 33.
[75]Somare (1975), p. 11.
[76]Rowley (1965), p. 157.
[77]Strelan (1977), p. 28.
[78]Fergie, Dean, 'Prophecy & leadership: Philo and the Inawai'a movement' in Trompf (1977), p. 172.
[79]Morauta (1974), p. 153.
[80]Young (1977), pp. 30–2.
[81]McGregor (1976), p. 207.
[82]Smith (1974), p. 136.

2

Between two worlds, two wars

The education policy of the missions was a modest one: it was confined to teaching basic literacy, and an appreciation of moral conduct. The literacy was necessary only insofar as it made Bible-reading possible; and the teaching of morals, chiefly by reference to the negative precepts of the Decalogue, was necessary to the civilising mission that the churches undertook. The education policy of the administration was still more modest. It consisted, at first, simply in teaching the natives to respect white men, because a white man could fell a black man with greater accuracy at longer range, and to more deadly effect, than a black man could fell a white. When a clan was subdued, the patrol officers (the Germans first, and then the Australians) appointed a 'luluai' – a native respected by his clansmen who would act as a paid agent of the administration. One obvious form of payment was the award of a black peaked cap, with a red band around it, and an official badge, and this was enough. It is unlikely that anything would have been appreciated more than this fancy piece of headgear. The grand-father of Topeni, a student from Goroka, was a luluai. The lesson of the gun was not lost on his clan, though it was only imperfectly understood. Topeni said:

This took place when the kiaps came to the Eastern Highlands first. Many people took part. They took [chunks of] limestone from the river, put them in bags, and carried them about. when it got dark, they stored them in a house which was specially made, and told children to keep away. Only young, strong men took part in this. They said if anyone was seen round the house they'd be shot with guns. Actually, they were pieces of wood shaped like guns, taken from the river. They imitated the Europeans. My grandfather took part. They told him he mustn't report it to the kiaps.

Once the 'kiaps' had taught the lesson of the gun, and stopped the natives fighting, they were more or less prepared to let the missions in to teach the lesson of love. Sometimes missionaries entered pacified districts as soon as the bill of health was posted. Elsewhere, the authorities discouraged mission activity, on safety grounds, for a longer than normal quarantine. The administration did not at first interefere in the educational work of the missions, but it gave them its tacit support; it certainly did not set up any schools of its own, unless these were to prepare the children of expatriates for schools 'down south'.

The standards achieved by the mission schools in the villages were, in Epstein's phrase, 'often minimal',[1] but then, they were never intended to be anything else. No one expected miracles when the 'children' who attended were in their 'teens, had never seen, read, or written a word of any language; who spoke a language with a hopelessly limited lexis and grammar that was, perhaps, spoken by no more than a few hundred other people; and who neither used, nor knew, a counting-system worth the name. They were as near as makes no difference to the tabula rasa of outmoded educated theory. It is really no wonder that the missions enjoyed an almost complete monopoly of primary education throughout the territory until well after the Second World War.[2] It was a responsibility that the missions took seriously. By the time the Pacific War broke out in December 1941, they could count a total of 90,000 pupils[3] in 2,500 mission schools.[4] The administration, by contrast, could boast a total of only 500 pupils, at a handful of schools, in and about Rabaul, run by, and on behalf of the expatriate community there. There were no administration schools in Papua at all.

The civil authorities were happy to leave schooling to the missions, and, in time, to subsidise mission expenses in the education field. Such subsidies came to be conditional, however, on the teaching of English. Burridge speaks of the native population as having been 'keen to learn Pidgin', not merely because this was the language in which the Europeans of the shipping companies and plantations addressed them, but because by learning this simple lingo, they could communicate with each other: Pidgin made them *'wantok'* (one talk), one tongue, one people'.[5] There were not wanting, missions and missionaries to gratify this preference; but there were those, too, who set their face against it. We have noted already that Sir William MacGregor commended the London Missionary Society for its English language teaching policy. Tomkins and Hughes report that the Anglican Mission, too, favoured English over the teaching of Pidgin, or Motu, in the zone allocated to it on the north-east coast of Papua from Cape Ducie to Mitre Rock. The bishop of this region took seriously the responsibility given to him by the authorities for abandoned children. He is said to have 'drawn' the whole coast from Samarai to Basilaki in quest of these 'mandated' children. In his Annual Report for 1907, the Bishop wrote: 'The dialects which the New Guinean mothers speak are many and diverse, so philologically the band of (fifty-seven) children is decidedly interesting. But it is intended that English is to be spoken'.[6]

Chatterton refers to the teaching of English to the Manu Manu people in the westernmost Motu-speaking villages. Subsidies to the mission there were awarded on the basis of pupil scores of fifty or over in an English test. Robert Lowe's 1862 system of 'payment-by-results' was alive and kicking in the colonies. Chatterton himself would have none of it. He continued to teach in the vernacular right up until after the Second World War, and, in his experience, and words, 'the curricula of most mission schools (and there were no others) were firmly based on vernacular literacy'.[7] The reason for his, and others' obstinacy was entirely conscientious: it was believed that children for whom there would be no more than primary education, could learn literacy of a meaningful sort only in their mother tongue. The administration was inclined to legislate for the select few who would manage to climb up (or be hauled up) into secondary schools in urban areas, rather than for the many who would not. In the same year (1907) in which the above-mentioned bishop wrote his annual report about language diversity in north-east Papua, the authorities declared: 'That the teaching of English be made compulsory in Mission Schools'.[8] School attendance had already been made compulsory, in theory, in 1897. Children between the ages of five and thirteen were required to

attend their nearest school for at least three days each week. Failure
to comply with this regulation would render their parents liable to
a fine of five shilllings, or a spell of three days behind bars. In
practice, the Governor might almost as well have outlawed
pneumonia.

Over and over again, the authorities laid orders for the ends,
without furnishing the means. The subsidy scheme was Governor
Murray's, but it was upheld by Glynn, the then Minister of State
for Home and Territories, on 16 May 1917. It was in this year
(regulations enforcing school attendance followed a ten year cycle)
that the punishment for default was imposed upon the children,
instead of – or rather, as well as – on their parents. Children
reckoned to be of school age who failed to attend regularly were to
be soundly whipped.[9] Dickson calls the subsidy scheme the
'response of a colonial governor denied metropolitan support', an
'education stop-gap' in under-resourced, under-committed times.[10]
He has no explanatory words for the whipping.

It was the view of the authorities in Australia both that a colony
should pay for its own administration, and that the missions should
conform to government policy.[11] Hence the drive towards monetisation, in the shape of the head-tax. Murray levied this tax –
ranging between five and twenty shillings per annum – only 'in the
more sophisticated districts'.[12] The revenue from this tax, introduced in 1919, was returned to the missions as subsidies to
education, on condition that English be taught, and that 'suitable
trades' and farming methods, be features of the school curriculum.
In the fifteen years between 1923 and 1937, annual expenditure on
the public service in Papua and New Guinea fell from 18,000 to
5,000 pounds sterling.[13] We might account for these figures by the
fact that there were few sophisticated districts in the territory at that
time, or by the conjecture that there were few pliable missions. But
a more likely explanation for them is that there were few parents
willng to deliver up their children to the unknown, and too few
agents of the law to administer all the fines and whippings that 'rule
by the book' entailed. A Grade Ten student, Kunual Karapia, offers
his father's experience as evidence that the authorities held to the
principle of compulsion, in spite of native reluctance (at that time,
and in one place at least) to rush to school:

When the first school was established in the village, the people refused
to send their children to school, because if they sent their children then
their life will be changed, and also they won't come back to their village
after gaining education. Their culture would be forgotten and they'd
follow the western ways. But the government encouraged the village
elders to force the parents to send their children to school. If the child
tried to run away from school, then the elders had to do something with
their parents.

It may look like hypocrisy on the part of the civil authorities,
when they made so little financial provision for the schooling in
which they affected such interest, especially when, after World War
One, the Australians promised to treat the natives better than the
Germans had done.[14] The German administration in New Britain
had established a school at Namanula for native children from
neighbouring islands; but this school, as Epstein points out, had
only just begun to produce its first graduates at the outbreak of
hostilities.[15] This school was not re-opened with the armistice,
though before the Second War, New Britain's four government
schools made this region more highly favoured than others: New
Ireland had one, and there was only one on mainland New Guinea,
in the Chimbu district.[16] The truth is that the administration was
on the horns of a dilemma: it could either subsidise mission
education, in the hope that as grants rose, standards would rise in
proportion; or it could build schools of its own, and control
staffing, curricula, and examinations as it saw fit. The Acting
Administrator, Brigadier-General T. Griffiths preferred the former
course. He proposed in 1933 that the missions be given responsibility for education throughout the territory, and that they be given
the means to build schools where they were wanting. In 1934,
Griffiths was replaced by Sir Walter NcNicoll as Administrator of
the Mandated Territory. No sooner had he settled into the post
than he revoked his predecessor's policy. He was unimpressed by
mission education, and was not satisfied that it could serve as the
foundation for a national system. It was not the least of his
misgivings about it, that many of the teachers were German
Lutherans whom he suspected were incompetent to teach, and to
teach in, English. Relations between the churches and the administration were understandably strained following the publication of
his critical report of May 1935.[17]

McNicoll felt unable to choose the other of the above two options, however, in view of what was called 'the definite hostility of Europeans towards the natives being given any education at all'. S. W. Reed went on (in an article published in 1943) to allege that: 'the exploiting class has a very real fear that intellectual training will make the native less amenable to labour.'[18] The missions may have come under suspicion from the government, but they came under overt attack from the planters. These were jealous of their economic hold on the natives, and feared that the missions were loosening it by teaching dangerously democratic ideas.[19] The conflict was very much a re-run of that between the mill and mine owners, and the British and Foreign Schools Society of a century before. What need had plantation labourers of literacy, what need of numbers – still less of training for self-supportive trades? To educate the natives was to spoil them, and to raise their expectations above obedience to the rules of the labour–contract, and compound. But not only planters opposed education as a 'ridiculous waste of public funds': housewives, warehousemen, ships' crews and law officers were heard to argue that the Melanesian mind was incapable of development much beyond the age of twelve.[20] These colonials (the citizens of an 'open society' – refugees, some of them from classist, hierarchical societies in Europe) were the first to see in cargo cults the seeds of nationalism and the desire for self-determination. They held the missions to account for sowing these seeds in their classrooms, or, at the very least, for tilling the soil by building and staffing them. A case like that at Yam, in the Madang district, where it was discovered (in 1938) that several pupils had been sent to the Lutheran Mission Central School expressly to learn the cargo secret, was adduced as evidence for this charge. It was not withdrawn, when one of the pupils was removed by his family for having learnt no such secret after four years' attendance.[21]

The administration found itself holding the ring between planters and missionaries. To have subsidised mission education, or to have established administration schools, would have antagonised the former; and to have done nothing would have antagonised the latter (and affronted international opinion, as well as the canons of responsible government). So it compromised without conviction, hesitated, and got lost. It felt it ought to do something for technical education, so it set up a technical school in the central highlands. By the time of the publication of the New Guinea Annual Report for 1939–40, fewer than ten of its graduates had secured artisan employment of a sort for which their training had fitted them, whilst sixteen graduates of the three-year course had returned to under-employment in the villages whence they had come.[22] Nevertheless, it was an administration school, not mission schools, that Buka Islanders wanted. They wanted a road from north to south of the Island, a government school, and an aid post. In Kiki's words: 'There were only mission schools, but no administration schools. There were no roads, no development schemes. Buka was a forgotten island'.[23] One is tempted to infer, in retrospect, that the putative superiority of government over mission schools was rather an article of faith than of fact. Certainly, the education offered by the missions was rudimentary. This was the word used by White in 1965, and by Read a year later. White dismisses it as follows: 'Pupils learnt a few Bible stories, the symbolic significance of which they failed to understand, picked up a little Pidgin, and were perhaps taught how to write their names in Roman characters.'[24]

But it is too easy to be dismissive. We can speculate about what might have been done, if the teachers themselves had had more schooling, if parents had been more supportive, if the missions had co-operated with each other, if they had taught English, if the accent had been on quality rather than quantity (there were 2,290 mission schools in the villages, in 1928). There are many 'ifs'. And the biggest of them must refer to the pitiful subsidies that the schools received. If the administration had been less concerned to appease the colonials, there is no saying what might have been done to make education more worthwhile. As it was, much of the blame for the inadequacy of the mission schools must lie with the civil authorities. And this is where the Permanent Mandates Commission of the League of Nations laid it. Members of this commission toured the territory in the 1920's and '30s, and in subsequent reports, were 'very critical of what they regarded as the slow expansion of the education system'. The meagre level at which subsidies were set came in for particularly frequent criticism, in view of the effort being made by certain of the missions to provide for the sort of trade-training and agricultural education of which the commission approved.[25]

Where the Commission found fault with mission schooling, was in its judgement that it was not as vernacular – not as well adapted to life in the rural areas – as it might be. The content of history and geography syllabuses, for example, was felt to relate too little to the local environment. It was too Europe-centred, too 'high culture'. In this connection, the more comprehensive judgement might have been made that the schools themselves were bush versions of German, Australian, and American schools, as if airlifted, syllabuses and all. Where language is concerned, it is difficult to see how the missions could have pleased all parties, all the time. They could hardly do right for doing wrong. The missions were commended not only for their essays in 'functional' education, but also for their use of local vernaculars.[26] In this respect, Chatterton could claim powerful backing for his resistance to administration inducements to use English. Yet Worsley reports what he calls a 'marked swing towards the Roman Catholic missions', in the 1930s (partly) on account of the teaching of Pidgin in catholic schools.[27] Perhaps Pidgin English was perceived by defectors to Rome to be a temporary way-station on the road to the real thing, or perhaps Pidgin was thought to *be* the real thing. Either way, the trend can have pleased neither Chatterton, nor the Commission. One of the commissioners reporting in 1939, a Miss Dannevig, threw doubt on the value of teaching pupils to read in any language at all, when there was no literature to be had, in or about the pupils' village homes. The lack of opportunity to read anything in the language of instruction, whether vernacular, 'Neo-Melanesian', or 'real' English, could negate years of primary schooling in as few seasons.[28] Only the missions were doing anything to make good this lack – and that for what secular commentators might think were the 'wrong' reasons.

In one district at least – one of the more 'sophisticated districts' referred to above – clients of the schools refused to be content to be taught in the master–slave language of the plantations. There had been Europeans in and about Rabaul for longer than almost anywhere else in the territory. The Tolai were, in consequence, more 'advanced' (in European terms) than other native peoples. They had had their education expectations raised, and dashed, by the opening and closing of the school at Namanula; they had accumulated shell-money in capital style; had availed themselves of whatever economic opportunities they were offered; and they had been among the first to reject *tambu*-money in favour of money that would 'buy goods in a European store'.[29] At the beginning of this chapter, we met Topeni's grandfather, the luluai. He became involved in a conspiracy to convert base limestone into silver:

> he thought they were dealing with real money. He knew it was limestones but he thought they'd be changed into money. At last a policeman named Yuma found out what they were doing, and reported to the kiaps. The kiaps sent policemen to arrest them. Next day they found themselves before the kiaps, and for their punishment they were beaten with cane sticks, and with their own gun sticks, and jailed for a month. After the month was over, they were released and told that in twenty years there'd be real money. My grandfather was given a small bag full of twenty cent coins to show him real money, what it was like. It was a small amount and worth less to my grandfather because money was not being exchanged as yet. This was before the days of trade stores.

Topeni goes on to tell how his grandfather kept the bag of coins, in spite of the advice of the village elders to throw it away because it was worthless. What follows is a curious reversal of conventional economic history:

> My grandfather kept it because he was told that in the future it would be useful. He kept it until shells were introduced into that area by the white men (in some numbers). Then he bought shells from the white men with the white man's money. The colleagues of my grandfather realised the limestones were useless, and they too made increasing use of shells.

Topeni's grandfather was beaten and imprisoned (and deprived of his luluai's badge) for being naïve, and credulous – for living near Goroka, in fact, in the highlands instead of near Rabaul, on the coast. This digression will serve to point up the cultural canyon that had opened up between the peoples of the coast, and those of the highlands: at about the same time as the Gorokans were being bedazzled by shells, the Tolai were turning to shillings and pence (not yet the cents of Topeni's recollections), and the means of earning them in the European manner. The people of Nodup demanded better education facilities. Not only this, they demanded education in undiluted, 100 degrees proof English. The elders of Nodup were not beaten and imprisoned for their impertinence;

their demands were gratified in the Waterhouse Memorial School.[30]

Willis says of the Laewomba people of the Huon Peninsula that they 'enjoyed fighting': it was both a sport, and a means of achieving personal status.[31] The same might be said of many tribes throughout the highlands and islands, and particularly the highlands. Where there were concentrations of Europeans; where there had always been an opportunity to engage in trade, and where now this opportunity was enlarged; where the missions and their schools had been longest established and there were openings in employment – in these 'sophisticated districts' the rule of law could be, and was, imposed sooner rather than later. Inland, and upland, pacification took time. The Papua Annual Report for 1922–3 speaks of 'the Papuan's craving for blood'.[32] This is a hard saying, but it is borne out in many descriptions given by missionaries, prospectors and explorers, of murder and mayhem on a grand scale. Food supplies failed on the celebrated expedition of Leahy and Dwyer along the Wahgi River: 'Many times they were forced away from the river, but whenever their guides led them back, they saw more dead bodies, more bones in the sand, all carried down from savage battlegrounds in the great grassed western valleys by the Wahgi'.[33]

This was in 1930. Four years later, the same Mick Leahy found the body of a prospector, murdered near Henganofi, in the Eastern Highlands. A District Officer and patrol officers rushed to the scene from Kainantu, to be attacked in their turn. The Annual Report for 1933–4 describes what happened in these words: 'During the fighting – one of the most desperate affrays recorded in the history of New Guinea, the District Officer and three members of his party were wounded with arrows, and nineteen of the attacking natives were shot dead before the remainder ceased fire, and made overtures for peace . . .'[34]

Life was cheap, and death a matter of no moment. The writer was right who judged that football and cricket would be reckoned poor substitutes for head-hunting raids.[35] But the authorities who encouraged the playing of these manly sports as a channel for frustrated energies and competitiveness cannot have foreseen just how warlike a simple game of football could be. Football played according to Australian rules is not a game for the faint-hearted, even at its most orderly, but the native ex-warrior contrived to

re-write the rule book in a language all his own. A game of 'futbol'
could take days to finish, and involve almost any number of
players. It would often be the result of a challenge between one
tribe or village and another, and its outcome was often decided by
the elders of the two groups, on the touchline. The game was over
when the score was even, or when the challenger's honour was
satisfied, or when the two sides had run out of substitutes.[36]

Spearsmen who could not be worn out on the playing-field
might be persuaded to wield a pick or spade. It was Murray's
earnest hope that he might make industrious workers out of
disappointed warriors, but the work that villagers were given to do
was not always in their own, or anyone else's best interests. Kiki
recalls how, in the 1920's, the Orokolo people were prevailed
upon to plant rice. Rice was the answer to fighting, malnutrition,
idleness, and import charges. So the people planted rice. Then,
'after a lot of work and effort they were told that their rice could
not be marketed'. Kiki goes on to describe how the government
persuaded the Orokolo people to switch to coffee. Coffee was the
answer to an indifferent market for rice, to idleness, and to foreign
exchange problems. So the people planted coffee. And once more,
says Kiki, 'the people worked for nothing. Their coffee could not
be sold.'[37] Of course, the government had other motives for
wanting the natives to engage in productive labour, besides
heading off tribal fighting: clerks, interpreters, houseboys, steve-
dores and manual labourers of all sorts were needed to keep the
white man's machines running smoothly.[38] It suited the administration to encourage rice and coffee growing; but the blow fell
upon the native growers, the duped of the earth, when these crops
failed. They lost the income they might have earned; they sacrificed
their staples for cash crops; and, they were denied the subsidies that
taxpayers elsewhere received. They enjoyed no income, so they
paid no tax, so they had no security for expenditure on the sort of
development that good boys earned. Education had to be paid for
by its consumers, like any other European 'good'.

But then, the authorities were diffident salesmen; they were soft
pedlars of education. Murray may have disliked head-hunters, but
he liked big heads only one degree better. Throughout this inter-
war period, it was an article of government policy that no
encouragement was to be given to the formation of a native élite.

The Administrator put the policy in the proverbial nutshell, in his Papua Annual Report for 1937–8, in words that smack of personal opinion – not to say prejudice: 'I may say at once that I am quite opposed to the creation of a Papuan intelligentsia, and would rather aim at the diffusion of an elementary education, with a knowledge of Engish.'

But in the expression of such a sentiment as this, Murray was only being the spokesman for the occupying power. Much of the legislation enacted in this period represented the generalised contempt in which the native population was held. The clothing regulations were only the most naked manifestation of this contempt. The missionaries had shamed women into wearing a 'meri' (Mary) blouse to cover their breasts, and urban Christians, with an acquired decorum, did so. They did so, that is, where law permitted; from 1920 onwards, until 1941, Papuans male and female were forbidden to wear any garment on the upper part of their body. Offenders were liable to a fine of between ten shillings and a pound, or to a term of imprisonment of between one and two months. In addition, the unlawful garment was to be destroyed,[39] with, one assumes, due ceremony.

The New Guinean (to whom the above regulation did not apply) could turn European ceremony on its head, not with the intent of mocking it, but of harnessing it to new ends. The prophet Mambu, of the Bogia people of Madang, made clothing one of the symbols of an influential cargo movement. In a home-spun version of baptism, men and women undid their grass and tapa-cloth bindings in front of him, so that he could sprinkle water on their genitals. He buried their tangled skirts and cod-pieces, and enjoined them to wear trade store clothes of European style.[40] That Europeans, whom the gods favoured, wore European clothes was evidence enough for Mambu that the gods scorned clothes of the old, rough cut. Europeans themselves hardly knew how, or whether, they should accept such a compliment; it depended on whether the likes of Mambu were being thought of as fools or knaves – whether that is, the book was being brought to them, or they were being brought to book. Before the Second World War, Papuans were being booked for wearing clothes (native or European) on their upper trunk; and after the war, they were being denied access to hotels and restaurants in Port Moresby, unless they wore a collar and tie, long trousers, and socks and shoes after six o'clock in the evening. Only the determination of Michael Somare (Chief Minister), in the 1970s, to visit the Davara Hotel on Ela Beach, Port Moresby, in his customary laplap and sandals, led to a softening (if not an end) of discriminatory clothing regulations.[41]

There was the same ambivalence about European attitudes towards cargoism: they swung from derision to 'panic opposition. Murray thought he had found the answer to what went on at Vailala in his charge of lunacy. He was Assistant Resident Magistrate at Kerema, in 1919, when it came to his notice that platforms loaded with food had been set up in certain villages, that big men were acting as masters of ceremony, that women were throwing off their clothes hysterically, that old men were dreaming dreams, and young men seeing visions. It appeared to be no exaggeration to call the affair, the Vailala Madness, and to put it down to an inferiority complex. When the movement persisted in spite of his mandarin abuse, however, Murray invoked a dormant law against 'spreading false reports'; after all, that self-styled prophets who promised the coming of ships and of Jesus Christ were doing this, was beyond dispute.[42] Murray's resort to a law of 1891 (designed originally to prevent the spread of rumours about massacres of white men, and thus undermine morale), set the pattern for the government's response to cargo movements between the wars. The law of 1933 which gave the Lt. Governor powers to declare any cult illegal was merely the setting down in cold print of an effective blanket ban.[43] We have already seen what rough justice was meted out to Topeni's grandfather, for his involvement in misguided alchemy in Goroka, before the Second World War. Mainia Tao, another student, cites his father's experience of cargoism in the Kainantu District, as evidence of the administration's condign way with 'troublemakers'. Tao was a boy of sixteen when the cult erupted in Arorata Village. When the local patrol officer got wind of strange goings on, he sent a policeman (a Chimbu) to the scene. The villagers overpowered the policeman, and captured his rifle. It is a matter of speculation what their punishment would have been if the villagers had not seized their chance to humiliate an old enemy, but had merely been found guilty of 'spreading false reports'. As it was, they suffered the unremitting force of penalties designed to deter. Mainia takes up the story:

> Three people reported what had happened to the patrol officer. The P.O. got some of his policemen and went up there with their rifles to fight these people. Luckily, these people didn't know how to use the rifle otherwise they might have shot the white man . . . They had a fight, and the white men and his policemen won and they bound the cargo-cult leaders with rope and brought them to Kainantu. They brought more than 30 people. They bound their hands, and beat them on the way (20–25 kms). They walked all the way with no food. They were put in prison. My father said they were there for 3 months. These were the first people to build the airstrip, by hand, not by any machine. They had to make a big cut. At first it was rugged, but then they made it flatter. It took them 3 months. The main road had reached Kassam Pass by this time, and some of them worked there, bringing up materials to build a permanent prison house.

Beatings, forced labour, mass imprisonment – these were by no means excessive-seeming punishments to people who had hunted heads, and who now wore, or left off, what they were told; who were taxed; who were subject to curfew regulations in urban areas; and who planted cash crops at the white man's say-so. All that Murray did was consistent with his words: '[The Papuan] is inferior to the European, and if we wish to avoid trouble, we should never forget this, and should never look upon him as a social or political equal.'[44] Murray sincerely believed that the black native was inferior to the white man, and so did Murray's white inferiors. They may have feared the black native, and it may have been fear that lay behind the White Women's Protection Ordinance of 1926, whereby natives were severely punished for molesting, or being suspected of intending to molest, white women.[45] But it was the contempt in which the black native was held that made such a regulation possible.

The natives were not unaware of this contempt, nor unmoved by it. The Papuans of Port Moresby were not so indifferent to where they lived, as not to question their expulsion to Koke, and the villages beyond the town boundary. (Only house-boys were permitted to live in boy-houses, and then they were subject to strict curfew.[46] The New Guineans of Lae were not so unmindful of the importance of land, as not to resent the loss of all their lands between the Markham and the Bumbu. (What was most frustrating was that they were ignorant as to how to press compensation claims, in a way that Europeans would respect.)[47] Native Christians on the Madang coast were not so innocent as to accept the white man's sermons about the brotherhood of man, without expecting the preacher himself to behave as a brother should. (Lawrence describes these church-people as having grown quite 'restive' by 1933.)[48]

The leaders of the 'Vailala Madness' favoured the use of German as an 'anti-government tongue' after the First World War, and the twelve-year long agitation as a whole has been interpreted as an expression of rebellion against the social and political position to which natives had been consigned.[49] In much the same way, the Second World War gave rise to comparisons between Americans and Australians – even at first between Japanese and Australians – that reflected the disdain with which natives felt themselves to have been treated by the latter. Asked by his employer why the natives had not 'stuck to' the Australians, as the Negroes had done to the Americans, one native employee replied: 'The American government taught the negroes to read and write, and so made it possible for them to understand all about the war. Our government gave us nothing. The little learning that we had came from the missions.'[50] This was precisely the 'little learning' that the planters and the politicans feared would be a 'dangerous thing'.

References

[1] Epstein (1969), p. 33.
[2] Lawrence (1964), p. 52.
[3] Louisson (1974), p. 110.
[4] Worsley (1970), p. 52.
[5] Burridge (1960), p. 265.
[6] Tomkins and Hughes (1969), p. 13.
[7] Chatterton (1974), pp. 17, 18, 50.
[8] 'Report of the R.I.C. Inquiry into the Present Conditions, including the Methods of Government, of the Territory of Papua, and the best means of their improvement, 1907', *Commonwealth Parliamentary Papers*, pp. cxxiv–cxxvi, in Jinks *et al.* (1973), p. 96.
[9] Wolfers (1975), pp. 24, 32.
[10] Dickson, D. J., 'Murray and education: policy in Papua, 1906 to 1964' in Thomas (1976), p. 31.

[11] Rowley (1965), pp. 92, 147.

[12] White (1965), p. 108.

[13] Lawrence (1964), p. 48.

[14] Threlfall (1975), p. 94.

[15] Epstein (1969), p. 24.

[16] Lawrence (1964), p. 48.

[17] McNicholl, R. R. (1969), 'Sir Walter McNicholl as Administrator of the Mandated Territory' in *Journal of the P. and N.G. Society*, Vol. 2, pp. 8–10, in Jinks *et al.* (1973), p. 282.

[18] Reed, S. W., 'The making of modern New Guinea', Philadelphia (1943), in ibid., p. 285.

[19] Threlfall (1975), p. 106.

[20] Hogbin (1951), p. 279.

[21] Lawrence (1964), pp. 88, 89.

[22] Nelson (1974), p. 77.

[23] Kiki (1968), p. 110.

[24] White (1965), p. 104.

[25] Barrington (1976), pp. 32, 33.

[26] ibid.

[27] Worsley (1970), p. 195.

[28] Palmer (1978), p. 9.

[29] Epstein (1969), p. 243.

[30] ibid., p. 253.

[31] Willis (1974), p. 30.

[32] *Papua Annual Report for 1922/3*, p. 15, in Jinks *et al.* (1973), p. 125.

[33] Sinclair (1971), p. 10.

[34] ibid., p. 22.

[35] *Papua Annual Report for 1922/3*, in Jinks.

[36] Read (1966), p. 150.

[37] Kiki (1968), p. 163.

[38] Tomkins and Hughes (1969), p. 81.

[39] Wolfers (1975), p. 47.

[40] Strelan (1977), p. 24.

[41] Clarke (1975), p. 6.

[42] Rowley (1965), pp. 162, 163.

[43] Wolfers (1975), pp. 22, 33.

[44] Dickson, D. J., 'Murray and education: policy in Papua, 1906 to 1941', in Thomas (1976), p. 23.

[45] Wolfers (1975), p. 58.

[46] Oram, N. D., 'Urban expansion and customary land', in Sack (1974) p. 173.

[47] Willis (1974), pp. 123, 124.

[48] Lawrence (1964), p. 87.

[49] Worsley (1970), p. 98.

[50] Hogbin (1951), p. 11.

3

The war of the worlds

Part I: The invasion

Cargo-cult expectations fused in a suggestive way with rumours of
war. Cult leaders had already drilled disciples with dummy rifles,
so impressive was white discipline. It was perfectly natural to make
an association of marching, rifle-slapping, and barked orders, with
a spell-binding control of cargo. And when white Australians were
seen to be marching, and slapping, and barking in ever greater
numbers, more frequently, and in more deadly earnest than ever, it
made sense to infer that something was afoot. Sanop, an ex-deputy
luluai of Gogohei village was only one of a long line of minor
prophets who looked to the coming of a ship laden with cargo for
all Melanesians. He promised cars, aeroplanes, and rifles, and
anticipated the return of the Germans half hopefully, and half
fearfully. Time had lent Germans enchantment – yet paradoxically,
the cry, 'Into the sea with the whites!' was raised.[1] Time had also
lent the Germans some colour. It did not take much to ignite cargo
frenzy in 1940. By then, news had reached native New Guineans of
fighting between the Germans and the British, so when a
missionary in the Madang district preached a sermon on the
Resurrection of Christ, there followed fits and prophesyings as if
on cue. A great darkness was predicted, and this in turn led to a
rush on the trade stores to buy hurricane lamps. Karkar Island – a
volcanic island off Madang – was said to be about to turn upside
down. It didn't do this, but what did happen was hardly less
dramatic. The dry season of 1940–1 broke all records in the

Madang area: it lasted for ten scorching months. The tropical vegetation was yellow, and the ground was hard and dry. Grass fires raged on all sides, like some vision of the apocalypse. A spark of the messianic cargo movement on Bagabag Island was carried by the wind to Karkar, where prophets named the day of the end of the world – January 1st, 1942. Labourers left the plantations to wait for the end, a planter rang for help to Madang, the police arrived, made mass arrests, and New Year's Day came and went.[2] But the prophecy was fulfilled to overflowing, in the sense that with 1942 came the Japanese: first the bombing, and then, by the end of that year, the occupation, first of Madang, and then of Karkar.[3] The promises and threats, the fires and prophecies, the drilling and the dreams all came together in noise, flight and jubilation. The Japanese were not the Germans, but the natives celebrated all the same.

In Orokolo, Kiki's people had identified the Germans with a word that they pronounced similarly, *Kiavani*, the local word for the dead. This in its turn was not very different from the way in which they said 'Japanese'. It was a short step from such verbal confusion to the assumption that the ancestors were about to return, bringing with them the cargo that they had been trying to bring for so long.[4] One of Vincent Eri's characters (in *The Crocodile*) is under a similar illusion: 'The Japanese are coming to help us (he says). They're going to make our lives easier. We will have cargo and be like the white men. The white men will work for us and then we'll be able to call them bastards for a change. We will make them wash our underpants and sweat for us for ten shillings a month.'[5]

Michael Somare's recollections of the Japanese are in the main favourable to them. He speaks of their having curried this favour with gifts of 'whisky in big bottles', biscuits and lollies, and of following up these gifts with something significant in the way of education. They tried to transplant education on the Japanese model, in the interests of mutual understanding, but bent most effort to persuading parents to release boys aged twelve to fifteen for education with military training. All was sweetness and light in the first weeks and months after the invasion, while the 'cargo' kept coming from Japan; but when this supply dried up, there was no more tinned fruit for the children at school. Then their parents had to collect firewood for the invaders, work for them, and provide them with food.[6] Schooling was one of the by-products of the invasion of Karkar Island, also: the islanders were taught Japanese (and were persuaded of the benefits of partnership in the Greater East Asia Co-Prosperity Sphere), and Japanese servicemen learned Pidgin English.[7] There is no evaluation on record of the relative progress made in these languages by the two groups.

On Buka Island, Bougainville, the Japanese made friends by encouraging ancestor worship – a practice congenial to them, as well as to the cult leaders who had exploited growing anti-European feeling in favour of the old religion. And even those who did not believe the cargo prophecies could not be unimpressed by the military strength of the Japanese.[8]

To other New Guineans, the Japanese were a mystery that came and went. Aizo Avese, a student from Hogaru village, Okapa, retails a memory of Sikola, a paternal uncle:

> The group of Japanese around my area made a tent-house just near the aid post, and Sikola thought they were his grandparents who had died before the war, so he killed a pig and brought it to them, and in return they gave him salt, axes, and necklaces . . . so he told the village people that their dead relatives were there. People from other villages also came to see the man who looked like their father, and grandfather. They brought food for them. After several times they moved away from that place. The people thought they had disappeared because they went during the night.

Down south in Port Moresby, where they were no Japanese, the presence of troops, he disbursement of rations and the sudden deployment of temporary buildings were a still bigger mystery. Papuans were engaged in large numbers as porters and labourers, but what they carried, and what they laboured to do could only be the subjects of the wildest speculation. They built the headquarters of the military administration at Konedobu, and they built several camps and a large base hospital outside the town limits. They cooked, they clerked and they served; they watched agape as 30,000 servicemen were victualled in one month alone; and they marvelled at the good things that flowed from the American commissariat in particular.[9]

That white men should be fighting among themselves (after so many years of preaching, and admonition) was a revelation in itself. They had railed against the loosing of arrows, and here they were dropping bombs and firing shells; they had moralised against the neglect of food gardens, and here they were levelling whole plantations; they had spared pennies for health and education projects, and here they were lavishing pounds on men and materials in the cause of war; they had preached the sanctity of life to village warriors, and here they were killing with abandon. The sermons, the court cases, the speeches and the schooling of a generation or more were discounted in a few short months. Never before had blacks been in such close contact with whites – the clothes regulations, the curfew, the apparatus of social segregation of colonised and coloniser broke down – and the two colours learned never to be forgotten lessons as they mixed. Ruhen puts it thus: 'Values painfully established over pitifully few years were overturned, and the Administrators could never look again to the native simplicity of acceptance in that degree which prevailed before the advent of the fighting forces.'[10]

An illusion was shattered: the white man was less than moral, and less than immortal. Close up, he was not very different from the black man. Indeed, many American soldiers were black men, who fought alongside white Americans on an equal basis. Negro soldiers supplied a role model to capture the imagination, and eclipse earlier models – the missionaries, the kiaps, the planters and the traders. The Manus islanders saw more American soldiers than most (Nelson speaks of nearly a million passing through the Manus base at one time or another),[11] and among these were a good few thousand Negroes. These Americans were generous to a fault. They seemed to possess so much of everything, that they cared little who owned it. The lithe children who had played and fished and dropped litter for Margaret Mead now ate ham and ice-cream at the hands of her countrymen. They wore jazzy American shirts, and wielded natty American tools. The cargo had come with a vengeance, and for the time being, few natives questioned how long it would stay.

Waste follows in the wake of plenty, perhaps, to a greater extent in war time than in peace. Papua New Guineans had never seen mechanical contrivances of such sophistication before – graders, diggers, bulldozers, artillery pieces, fighter planes, landing craft, and wireless equipment – nor had they ever seen such prodigality.

Hulks littered the bays, and abandoned villages, like blown dinosaurs. They witnessed, as Rowley says, the 'wholesale destruction of vehicles, buildings, furniture and supplies of all kinds'.[12] How much more of all of these things there were where all was so 'easy come easy go', the native hardly dared dream. America came to be seen as the land from which the cargo came, via Sydney, perhaps, but in the first place from America. The same largesse dispensed in Samoa had the same effect. The novelist Albert Wendt has Lenigao return to his village after a long absence, bearing 'cargo', whose source is the local American air-base.[13] The open-handedness of the GI in the Second World War turned many a Pacific head, with consequences uncalculated at the time, and incalculable now.

More important than that the American soldiers treated the natives with generosity, though, was that they treated them as equals – 'as brothers and as human beings', in Worsley's phrase.[14] The Australian New Guinea Administrative Unit (ANGAU – the emergency military government during the war) did its best to prevent fraternisation between the natives and the Americans, but in the Milne Bay Area, at least, the attempt only served to make areas 'out of bounds' more attractive. The English-speaking Papuans educated at Kwato were particularly impressed by the cultural *savoir-faire* of the American Negroes.[15]

It was during the war that the Australian administration made its first positive moves into the fields of health and education.[16] The secondary, and later teacher-training institution, at Sogeri (the nursery of more than one future, indigenous Cabinet Minister) was established at this time, and larger sums of money than ever before were allocated to social and economic projects. The heightened sense of responsibility for the two territories on the part of the administration, was the consequence of at least three considerations: the help that the natives had given to the allies, particularly in Papua; the damage and injury that the natives had sustained; and the necessity to counteract Japanese propaganda, and perhaps also the criticism of the Americans (and others who had seen the primitive state in which the natives still lived, after so many years of Australian trusteeship) that the administration had dragged its feet. The League of Nations had upbraided the Australians for its benign neglect in the inter-war years; something must be done to ensure that a successor organisation was not given the same grounds for finding fault.

The Minister responsible for overseas territories had used a phrase in 1943 – 'The Fuzzy-Wuzzy Angels' – that was meant to convey approval, affection, and thanks. It was patronising (we might even call it 'racist'), but it was approving and affectionate nonetheless. 'The Fuzzy-Wuzzy Angels', he had said, 'have been the victims of shoddy treatment and will require a comprehensive plan of social betterment.'[17] According to a number of army commanders, these 'angels', dressed as carriers and stretcher-bearers, had been the critical factor in the retreat on the Kokoda Trail, in the retrenchment and ultimate victory.[18] This was the generous appraisal of the contribution made by the fuzzy-wuzzies, some time after, and some way away from, the events themselves. It was sometimes forgotten that these angels had been pressed men; Worsley describes 'sick wastage' among native carriers on the Kokoda Trail, as having been 'thirty per cent at its worst'.[19] In addition, malaria and dysentery were introduced into areas of the Highlands that had not known these diseases. It has been calculated that in all, some fifteen thousand Papuans and New Guineans died as a direct result of the hostilities – the grass trampled by the battling elephants of the proverb. Twenty thousand buildings had been destroyed, and one hundred thousand pigs had been killed or commandeered.[20] When we add to these quantified losses, the displacement of large numbers of men, the breakage of contracts, the interference with customs and trade and the scattering of families and clans, we can begin to appreciate what impact the war had on its pacific hosts. Australian gratitude was real enough, and there is no reason to doubt the sincerity of the administration when it promised reparation for the 'shoddy treatment' the natives had received. A. J. Ward, the Minister for External Territories, represented the view in a speech in the Canberra parliament, in 1945:

> Apart from the debt of gratitude that the people of Australia owe to the natives of the Territory, the Government regards it as its bounden duty to further to the utmost the advancement of the natives and considers that can be achieved only by providing facilities for better health, better education and for a greater participation by the natives in the wealth of their country and eventually in its government . . .[21]

Some of this concern was undoubtedly 'propagandist'. The Nigerian novelist, Chukwuemeka Ike describes, in his novel *The Potter's Wheel*, how a Mobile Cinema Van came to his village to show propaganda films in which the British trounced the Germans;[22] and John Munonye, another Nigerian (in his novel *Obi*) refers to the hope of one Willie, an ardent nationalist, that Britain would be defeated in the war, and so leave Nigeria to itself.[23] Vincent Eri attests to a similar debate among villagers in PNG, about whose side they were on. Hoiri the schoolboy and English-speaker favoured the Australians; older men who had experienced the Australians as colonialists over many years were less sure.[24] Undoubtedly, there was every possibility in some areas that villagers would transfer their loyalties from their old masters, to new ones whose ships and planes had bigger holds; and the possibility persisted until the outcome of the war was beyond doubt.

Development projects were planned to counteract the propaganda of the cargo cult leaders, as well as that of the Japanese. It was far too early for those who witnessed the landing of all sorts of mechanical novelties during the war, to make the connection between these, and study, and passing examinations, and working from nine o'clock until five. The natives of the Eastern Highlands caught not only malaria and dysentery, they caught what came to be called the 'Ghost Wind', from a germ carried up the Kassam from the Markham Valley. It began in 1943 with the construction of cargo houses, and drilling with dummy rifles. These houses were filled with sticks and stones and waste articles of all sorts, which it was supposed would turn into consumption goods of the sort that were dropping from planes, and being transported by lorry daily up and down the Markham. Five thousand feet up the Kassam, villagers had heard the planes droning, and had felt the wind of the flailing knife of war. But they had not experienced the abundance of goods – they had not been the recipients of Japanese or American gifts – that had been what the war meant to the villagers about Rabaul or Madang. On the contrary, the trickle of European goods into Kainantu and Goroka, of the pre-war years, now all but dried up, and the Eastern Highlanders were left to their own devices. These devices included much speculation, much prophecy, much marching, and much apocalyptic shivering and shaking.[25]

Paliau's movement, on Manus Island, was a product of his reflections on the massive American occupation and its aftermath. He observed the emphasis that the Americans placed on elementary hygiene, on the orderliness of their camps, and on their easy, good-neighbourly ways. Paliau was sure that the future for his countrymen lay in a complete break with the haphazardness of the village economy, and all the indiscipline and factiousness of the past; it lay, instead, in a faithful imitation of American standards and habits, and in work. He preached improved sanitation, monogamy, and the abandonment of trade in dogs' teeth, bridewealth, and burial feasts.[26] Paliau's system was a compound of sound sense, neo-Catholic utopianism, and cargo mysticism. This last came to the fore in his movement for a time (when the authorities ignored his overtures for assistance, or were openly hostile), but Worsley stands up for him: 'Paliau's feet were well on the ground,' he says. Allegations of cargoism levelled at Paliau's movement were misdirected; the flecks of mud on Paliau's European clothes had been kicked up by an out-and-out cargo cult called 'The Noise'.[27] Paliau himself gave no encouragement to the wilder doctrines and manners of the leaders of the 'Ghost Wind', 'Noise', 'Wislin', 'Mambu', and other millenarian cults. If he crossed swords with the authorities it was because they gave him no encouragement in his perfectly sane endeavours, with the result that he felt obliged to seek a political solution of his own. There is no question of his having 'spread false reports' in any seriously seditious way. But it was only after his arrest and imprisonment on this old charge, that officials sought to educate him in the ways and means of village democracy, and of establishing development projects on a sound economic footing. They chose the path of co-operation in 1951 only after they had tried Paliau's patience and good faith over some years.

Yali of Madang had received his education in the white man's methods of production, during the way, in the white man's own land. He did not avoid Australian disapproval, legal charges and a spell in prison; but then he did give the authorities more cause for doubting his motives, and leadership qualities, than Paliau. He was more in love with power for its own sake than his contemporary; what is more, he was quite illiterate. In consequence, he had access only to the externals of western culture, its genesis and evolution were a closed book. Promoted to the rank of Sergeant of Police, he was drafted to Queensland for a six-month training course. There, in Cairns and Brisbane, his eyes and ears were opened to sights and sounds undreamt of in his cargo philosophy. He understood – or he appeared to understand – that these things were got by hard work, and by an efficient division of labour,[28] not by marching, or by shaking, or by decking tables with white cloths and jugs of flowers. He could return to Madang, and pour out his impressions and perceptions to patrol officer McCarthy, in these gladdening words:

> The people of New Guinea are lazy, thriftless, unhealthy and dirty. They plant only enough food for bare existence, work only a few hours a day, and so waste the land that God has given them. They are filled with self-pity, comparing their poverty with the many things the white man has, but they do not do a single thing to help themselves by work . . .
>
> I have seen how the white man lives in his own country. He has good houses, much food and he obeys the law. Every day, except on Sunday, he goes to work and earns money to buy the things and food he wants.[29]

McCarthy must have thought European culture had made a convert; at any rate, he was enthusiastic enough about Yali's confession to take it down word for word. 'Every man and woman in New Guinea must work, otherwise we will remain for ever backward.' What more can a patrol officer have wanted to hear? What more effective ambassador for the cause can he have hoped to find than a born-again cultist – a man of parts blinded by the truth on the Damascus Road? The authorities leaped at the chance, and appointed Yali to be an agent of propaganda for the work ethic in the villages. Under his leadership, villages were combined in more efficient units, like army camps, houses were built in straight lines, and latrines were dug.[30] All seemed set fair, until local people misinterpreted Yali's intentions, and he himself broke with church observance, and lent his support to the men's cult in his home village. Thus, by the time Paliau was falling foul of the civil authorities for 'spreading false reports', Yali was being accused by hostile Christians of imprisoning people, and inciting to rape.[31]

Tommy Kabu (born Koivi-Aua) was another native policeman to whom the war gave an accelerated, highly-charged education in western development methods. He travelled still farther afield than

Yali, to Cairns, Brisbane, and Sydney. Travel, indeed, was added
to the repertoire of factors contributing to great expectations of a
material sort, in these and other men. It combined with pre-war
Christianity, mission education, and wartime abundance, in an
urge to secure for PNG, goods enjoyed (it seemed) by almost all
but their countrymen. Japanese and American soldiers prised open
the lock of the strongbox of secrets that missionaries, teachers,
planters, and kiaps had kept so tight shut for so long, and travel
blew the lid off for good. Of the three men considered here,
Tommy Kabu was the most far-sighted in his proposals for change.
He came from the Purari Delta, and his programme was firmly
founded on the potential for economic development in that district.
He returned from Australia with a firm belief in the necessity for
co-operative methods of farming and marketing cash crops. If he
was distracted by an impatience with the trappings of the old
religion, and by the paraphernalia of European-style offices, full of
desks and papers,[32] his essential vision of the possible was not
blurred. His determination to do away with the piercing of the
septum, with male initiation, betel-nut chewing, and houses built
in the traditional style may not have been better advised than that of
the missionaries before him,[33] but in that the villagers were
themselves dissatisfied with the old ways, and ready and willing to
adopt the new, Tommy Kabu was preaching to the converted.
Perhaps in stirring, even revolutionary times, piece-meal reforms
would have been blown away.

Paliau, Yali, Tommy Kabu, Kondom in the Chimbu, and others
elsewhere – the 'New Men' Rowley calls them, men whose lives
were changed by a rapid succession of hallucinogenic events and
experiences – these were the descendents of the luluais appointed by
the authorities of the past, and the predecessors of the politicians
chosen by the electors of the future. They were the N.C.O.s of the
citizen army in the post-war, pre-independence years, the men
most attentive to the wild promises of progress made at passing-
out parades all over the country. Lawrence quotes a European
officer as having said to Yali and his fellow recruits: 'In the past,
you natives have been kept backward. But now, if you help us win
the war . . . we Europeans will help you . . . (You will have)
houses with galvanised iron roofs, plank walls and floors, electric
light, and motor vehicles, boats, good clothes, and good food

. . .'[34] When promises were made of this sort, who needed to lead
or join a cargo cult? Who wanted to dream dreams when the reality
was within reach? The promises were conditional of course; an
allied victory was still so uncertain in 1943 that bribery of this sort
could appear quite harmless, and be quite easily justified. Victory
might indeed have been so glittering a prize as to make all things
seem possible thereafter. But the conditions were met: Yali and his
friends the 'Fuzzy-wuzzy angels' did help the allies win the war;
and the promises were made all over again. McCarthy himself calls
them 'ridiculous', and 'so lavish as to be impossible of redemption'.
'The rosy future' he says, 'would provide schools for all, hospitals
near every village, and food in abundance.' The point that some
self-help was also required (the very point that Yali and Tommy
Kabu had brought back from Queensland) 'appeared mostly to
have been missed'.[35]

Vincent Eri puts the following speech into the mouth of a
departing Australian at the end of the war: 'The King is pleased.
For this he has many things in his mind that he wants to do for you.
He plans to open up many schools for your children. As well as
this, co-operative societies will be formed in each of your villages
to show you how to run businesses.'[36] It was just such a speech that
no less a dignitary than the commandant of ANGAU, Major-
General B. M. Morris, made at the war's end – such a speech as
some Papua New Guineans memorised, and recited verbatim, until
the eve of independence of 1975.[37] It was understandable that those
who listened to such speeches took them seriously, and set store by
them. At the time, they were intended to. They could not have
been expected to realize, at the time, that Major-General Morris
and his junior officers were flushed with success, that these men
were not politicians, and that therefore they should not be held to
account for their over-explicit expressions of gratitude. The
officers themselves could not be expected to know that promises
made in English, of a vague and expansive kind, would be made
simple, and concrete, and memorable in Pidgin and Police Motu;
their audiences were accustomed to accepting spoken words at their
face value – words did not need signatures and seals to give them
meaning. It was only when the actions of the Australian authorities
did not speak louder than their words, after the war, that Paliau,
Yali, Tommy Kabu and the rest took action of their own. The

reversion to pre-war forms of worship and organisation, to mimicry and formula, was the work of bitter, frustrated, desperately disappointed men. If they had themselves understood that hard work was going to be necessary if the promises were to be kept, they could not preach this message, or sustain their preaching, in the long term. The villagers had not understood; they had not been to Brisbane or Sydney, and been taken in hand by anthropologists and administrators; if they had received any education at all, it had been a truncated mission education of the sort that laid stress on the religious element in European culture. They were credulous and impatient. They could ask their leaders when the promises would be redeemed; they could doubt whether this would ever be; and they could infect their leaders with this doubt. Their leaders were men. They could sense betrayal, and their loss of credibility. Back home, in the vernacular, they could as easily, and as lightly, put off European clothes, as they had put them on.

Part 2: The aftermath

A Grade eleven student, A. S. Hilly, with a more sophisticated command of English than some of his fellows (and an ambition to write professionally) described the post-war scene as follows:

> The bloody war ended and the natives returned to their villages with the invasion of cargo cult beliefs in their minds. While, as partakers of the war, they had been wondering where the Australians and Americans obtained the goods to feed their soldiers.
>
> In their respective villages, the returning natives gathered together their fellow men and discussed the origin of the cargoes and how they could obtain them. With great enthusiasm these returning natives encouraged the confused ones to back them up and participate in the cargo rituals.
>
> Perplexed, they searched for cargo everywhere – the ancestral spirit dwelling places, the river banks and even graveyards; and gradually it became a common human endeavour.

It became just as common to dust off the belief that the white man was keeping back cargo that was the rightful property of the Papua New Guinea native. The Allies had given much in the war, but no more than was due – indeed they had given much less than was due. To villagers who believed that all good things came from the ancestors, it was natural to think that the Americans and Australians had acted as agents of the ancestors. Their preaching of the work ethic was an exercise in deception. Paulias Matane (who realised his ambition to write professionally) recalls his father giving vent to these convictions:

> The war is over now. To hell with the Japanese. There is a lot of food given to us by the Australian and American soldiers. This includes thousands of cases of tinned meat, bags of rice, flour, sugar and other things which I have not seen and eaten before. They have also left truckloads of clothes. We are very lucky. We will not need to work in the gardens and wear these torn clothes. Ah, thank you, Australia and America. We needed your help . . . but you used to stop our cargo from our great grandfathers. The food and clothes you now give us is (sic) only a small portion of what was put in big houses by our great grandfathers.
>   Our great grandfathers are working hard making clothes, cars, trucks, food, and many things for us. These white people are stopping these things from reaching us and are keeping them for their own use.[38]

The suspicion of European perfidy was of long standing. It had always been necessary for large ships to await a favourable tide before negotiating the gap in the coral reef, and sailing into Port Moresby.[39] Mambu is only the best known of those who asserted that Europeans spent these hours of waiting changing all the labels on the crates.[40] One Batari put the assertion on a new, and firmer footing, when he chanced upon a crate bearing the label 'Battery'. He had education enough to recognise the similarity to his name, and nerve enough to claim that he was the intended recipient. So much a 'fact' did it become, that Eri could entwine it in fiction: he has Aravape say: '(Ships) stay outside the reef for a couple of days while the goods in the hull are renamed. They change your name and mine on all the goods that our dead ancestors send for us.'[41]

This belief was merely the concrete expression of a general feeling after the war, that Papua and New Guinea had been let down. Yali evinced this feeling in its most acute form: he learned the bitter truth from an officer in Port Moresby, that the promises made to him by the recruiting officer in Brisbane, back in 1943, had been 'wartime propaganda'. Yali's bitterness was very great, says Lawrence, 'His whole war service and loyalty to Europeans had been a mockery'.[42] It was out of just this sense of having been betrayed, that cargoism grew in the late 1940s, and spread, until its blossoms filled every corner of the country. Yali took his own frustration out on the missions: he abandoned church-worship himself, and intimidated others into doing the same. Though he had to use strong-arm tactics to persuade catechists to desert the church, his anti-mission campaign and his restitution of the native Kabu ceremony found many sympathisers among those whose attachment had never been more than mercenary. The novelist Onuora Nzekwu writes of such people in Northern Nigeria: 'We found them and their sermons unattractive and boring; but still we went and listened to them because at the end of each religious service or lecture, they distributed dresses, bottles of kerosene, heads of tobacco and items of household use to us.'[43] When such items ceased to be distributed – when, indeed, they were withheld – then, there was no further need to listen to the boring sermons. Even before the war's end, white missionaries had apprehended a growing antagonism among those they had counted among the sheep. Batari had led his followers in attacks on the Catholic and Methodist missions in Nakanai, had tied up and beaten a Catholic priest, and chased students out of the Methodist Circuit Training Institution at Malalia.[44] Father Holland of Sehaparete had been knocked to the ground when he had preached against false expectations of cargo.[45] Now that the war was over, there seemed to be very little to hope for from further church-going, money offerings, and prayer. Even schools, district offices, and police stations came under attack from the new breed of militant cultists, and the attacks persisted right up into the independence period, in the late 1970's.[46] Being anti-government, the rebellion was also anti-tax, and anti-council. Among the eight points in the programme of the cult leader Mangring, were these:

- people who join a local government are sinners. They will not have eternal life.
- those who stand firm against council temptations will see the face of God in heaven.
- it looks as if the administration will ask us to pay fees for our children's education in a few years' time. Send your children to school but do not pay fees.[47]

Europeans learned to recognise the signs of impending, or actual cargo movements. They tended to exhibit one of two sets of characteristics: either villagers tore off European lendings, and reverted to the old observances and to the bush; or they denied the past, and decked themselves and their villages with the trappings of the white man. The former course often involved destruction and privation. The egregious Batari, for example, required of his followers that they destroy their food gardens, cut down coconut trees, slaughter all pigs, dogs and fowls and leave them to rot, uneaten; houses were to be torn down, and villagers were to sleep in the open, on the ground, come rain or come dry. The object of this self-inflicted suffering was so to affect the spirits as to force them to reclaim the cargo from the white man, on the sufferer's behalf.[48] The abandonment did not always call for immediate acts of self-denial, however; just as often, the cult prophet licensed a Shrove Tuesday of free spending and excess. The pigs might be slaughtered, but they might then be gorged upon at day-long and night-long feasts. European money might be discarded, but it might buy all that the trade stores had to sell first. Lent would come later, to be followed by the coming of the cargo, and the end of suffering, on the cult equivalent of an Easter morning.[49] Other, less dramatic – but no less telling – signs of the 'negative' cults, were empty schools, empty churches and a more than usually obvious reluctance to work. One is reminded of the Academies of Projecters in Gulliver's Lagado.

On the surface, the 'positive' cults would be welcomed and embraced by the established order. The signs of these might include neat, 'European' dress, well kept gardens, church attendance, the ritual imitation of school and office procedures and the buildings of would-be wharves and airstrips.[50] Common among the trappings, or stage properties of these 'positive', play-acting cults, were suitcases, vases of flowers, and tables spread with cloths. A Grade ten student, Aizo Avese, begins his re-telling of a cargo story in these words:

> In other areas like Kainantu and Goroka, cargo cult people said if you put flowers on top of a suitcase, it will fill up with money. Hane Ano tried to perform this cargo cult. He told the village people that they must build a new house, so they worked hard and built a new house. After that, he told them, according to your suitcase you will get a big

amount. Also if you bring a lot of money, you will get a lot of money. So he asked them and he brought their suitcases and he filled the suitcases with his clothes and put the money on top. He asked one man to come and see if the suitcase was filled up. Other suitcases were empty but only one, on top of it there was the money that they brought him, to make it look full. He told them to see with their eyes and not their hands.

The confidence trickster from the town practised his deception on one ingenuous village after another, learning when to stop, and when to move on. In Catholic areas, red wooden suitcases were highly favoured, similar to those used by priests for holding the elements for the mass.[51] When Jim Taylor demonstrated the new money to Eastern Highlanders after the war, he laid the notes and coins out on a table, spread with a cloth, and covered the whole with glass.[52] Suitcases, vases of flowers, cloths, papers, and of course money, were to all appearances potent symbols for the white man, so they were bound to be the symbols of hope for the black. Indeed, they were not symbols only; one of my more aged Grade ten students, Louis Peter, relates how young men went as contract labourers after the war, to coconut and rubber plantations on the coast:

> After the contracts were completed and when they came back, they came carrying red wooden suitcases. In them, there were lots of things like shirts, shorts, sea shells, mirrors, soap, one shilling coins etc . . . which we had never seen before. When the government put the first schools in our area, coastal teachers were sent there. The teachers told us that if we put our children in school, after six years of schooling, they will be sent to the coast. When we were told that . . . we thought of the red box full of new things which were brought from the coast by the young men.

This was no deception; this was no confidence trick. This (albeit humble) cargo was real. If any unfortunate association was set up, it was that between this (or similar) cargo, and six years of schooling. But at least the act of sending children to school was a vehicle for the hope, rendering unnecessary acts of an irrational, ritual kind.

Another vehicle for hope was business development. At its lowest valuation, 'bisnis' was a cargo cult that could be seen to 'work'. But again, it was rational, and, unlike schooling, obviously

productive. Finney describes at length how Goroka came to be a
centre of the coffee-growing industry. A latter-day belief in
sympathetic magic made Gorokans keen to welcome Europeans
among them – even land-owning Europeans, who would make
immediate cash payments for the land, and share the profits of
partnership with the most enterprising.[53] The Gorokans proved, in
fact, to be more enterprising than most indigenes so soon after first
contact. They spent their new money less on the consumer
durables to which they now had access, than on investment goods,
such as coffee-processing equipment, commercial vehicles, retail
and catering businesses and agricultural projects. This preparedness
to invest had a lot to do with local perceptions of status.[54] Finney's
work is about the Gorokan version of the 'big man', but Sack
confirms Finney's view that the opportunity (presented by the
novelist and District Commissioner, Ian Downs) to participate in
the cultivation of cash crops, brought a perceptive 'change in native
attitudes to land'.[55]

Elsewhere, development projects tended to be cargo cult and
business enterprise all in one. Tommy Kabu's 'Kompani' is the
classic case of such a combination of wish and work. In that
ceremonial buildings were destroyed, along with the masks and
drums of the old religion, the movement was of the 'positive' type,
as defined above. But in addition to houses being built in
'suburban' straight lines, villagers were persuaded to work together
in a quite unprecedented way, growing and marketing cash crops,
and, for a time, reaping respectable profits.[56] Yali's movement was
one that began life as an Australian-backed development project,
and degenerated into an anti-Australian cargo cult;[57] whilst the
Johnson Cult, at first a maverick political movement (whose object
was to secure cargo by electing US President Johnson to the House
of Assembly), later became a development agency with its feet,
more or less, on the ground. Cultism and politics were combined
in another celebrated movement: that of Yaliwan of Yangoru.[58]
Indeed Strelan could write in 1977: 'Cargoism, politics and business
have become inextricably interwoven on Bougainville, just as they
have in Madang, Lae, the Sepik, and other parts of Melanesia.'[59]
Cargoism, commercialism, reason and religion fused in expectations that might centre on worship, education, electioneering, or
business, by turns, or in fertile combination; and this in spite of

repeated attempts by the administration to teach the economic facts of life.

The teaching took two forms: on the one hand selected adults were taken on short-term, educational visits to Australian farms and factories; and on the other hand, large numbers (yet still a minority) of children were given primary (and a still smaller minority, secondary) education, in which the principles of 'self-reliance' were taught, and put into practice in classrooms, dormitories and food gardens. Several prominent Papuan and New Guinean natives were spirited away by plane to Australia, to be shown how raw materials are processed in the white man's factories, to emerge as the finished products that blacks had supposed appeared by magic. 'No efforts were spared,' acording to Ruhen, 'to demonstrate the processes by which civilised man accumulates his vast riches of consumer goods'.[60] The motives of the tour leaders were unimpeachable; yet they may have over-estimated the powers of their charges to assimilate so much so soon. Machines that turn out parts for radios by the minute are no less 'magical' than men who do these things by the hour. Stent refers to one J.K., who had received both an education of the long-term, school-based kind, and who had spent five months on an in-service training course in New South Wales. He was a clerk for several years, working with Rural Progress Societies for the Department of Agriculture. He spoke and wrote good English, and was 'very competent with figures'.[61] Yet this J.K. was assistant to L.K., himself a former Catholic Catechist, educated, anglophone, in the Peli association of Maprik. The main emphasis of this cult, the brainchild of Yaliwan of Yangoru, was, in Stent's words, 'the miraculous manufacture of money'. There is no doubting the eagerness for education in the post-war period; what *is* in doubt is whether the encouragement given to it by the authorities served to mitigate cargo tendencies, or to exacerbate them. It is true, education objectives were long-term. But the promises made, and the teaching delivered, were offered (like a party political mani-festo) to the unschooled of an age to vote – the parents who would build the school; who would pay the fee; and judge the result. Kondom, president of a newly formed co-operative society in Chimbu, handed eight rules as on tablets of stone, to an enthusiastic audience. The eighth rule was: 'The best and most important one is education'. The audience roared its approval of progress, as might have been expected.[62] A Grade ten student, Sion Akwanda, describes other such parents in the Eastern Highlands:

> They thought sending their children (to school) would mean that their children would be taught western ways of life and tricks. Some thought that their children would gain the white man's knowledge and they would help them fulfil their expectations about cargoism. Then one day they would get rid of the whites, gain power and chase the whites away, and even they would occupy the white men's high-covenant houses and be like whites.

It might be objected that parental, and community, misapprehensions of education were unavoidable; that they were a small price to pay for the longer-term understanding of the (above-mentioned) economic facts of life, on the part of the pupils themselves. But it is far from certain that even ten years of formal schooling – four of them in boarding high schools – was enough to efface, or overprint, unrecorded ages of cultural conditioning. What lies behind these words of another Grade ten student, Kipave Tabefa?

> They saw the whites every time eat their food only from the house. The people wondered where they got it from. They thought their gateway was the river. So they thought if we sent our children to school they will teach them how to get all these things which the whites are having.
> So they sent their kids into school. When they went to school in grades one to six, some of them were selected and went to high school. Later, when these people graduated they told their parents that the education is not like that. It is a place where they get knowledge and get jobs to earn money.

As his teacher, I cannot be sure that Kipave had 'understood' what I understand by education. The mature Louis Peter, for all his European name, and European clothes, was another student about whom I have my doubts. He told a long story about how his cousin had had visions, and had conversations with a returned ancestor, a European dressed in black whom he had 'conjured' in a 'square house' in the dark. Louis had been given to believe that he was listening to the voice of Bemori, his cousin's adopted son, now dead.

- The voice was coming from the square house.
- Do you believe, now, (I asked) that you were listening to Bemori's spirit?
- Yes, I still believe.

Louis later transposed his belief into the past tense.

> Most of the villagers believed in it, and I did. I thought after I'd been to school, I'd come back and be the clerk (of the cult). During 1974 missionaries came; they discouraged the people. They said my cousin was telling lies. But myself, I really believed in my cousin, because I saw the Europeans and heard the way they spoke. Now, I believe the missionaries, because I came to high school, and church, and asked questions, and I was told it was done by the power of Satan.

Was Louis Peter any the wiser for being told this? Had ten years of education merely substituted Satan for the spirits of the ancestors? Again, it might be objected that in any society, no more can be hoped for from ten years' worth of schooling, than the sketch of an understanding of 'what education is', and of the differences between physics and metaphysics. But Papua New Guinea in the 1950s was a society in which cargo-thinking was deep-rooted; indeed it was the very soil. Epstein cites Worsley's contention that cargoism was a rural phenomenon, mere paganism, and that it was unknown, for example, among the sophisticated Tolai about Rabaul. Yet Epstein recalls a time, in the course of his own field-work, when 100 young men abandoned their villages to wait in a camp for the coming of a submarine that would take them to America.[63] And Clarke's more recent research finding is that 'belief in the power of the Sorcerer is universal, even amongst college and university students'.[64] Strelan came to the following carefully considered conclusion, in 1977, after much research into the 'history and theology of cargo cults': 'The idea is propounded that, with opposition from the government and the church, supported by a planned educational drive and economic development, cargo cults and cargo thinking will gradually disappear. These, however, are oversimplified solutions based on a superficial analysis of a complex problem.'[65]

Beliefs of a cargo sort were held more or less extremely, and expressed more or less explicitly by villagers, parents, pupils and students. They were not always enshrined in outward ritual, or institutionalised in a named, located movement. They were, and are, endemic in Melanesian thinking. The externals of cargoism were more obvious among pre-literate villagers who thought that to use English would itself crack the code; but the beliefs persisted in pupil ambitions that were no less materialistic than their sponsors'. If the latter believed in 'instant transformation',[66] the former accepted that there would be a delay of six, eight or ten years before they could come into their inheritance of well paid jobs and high-covenant houses. So long as there have been provocative disparities between the power and wealth possessed by whites and blacks respectively, so long have there been soil conditions favourable to the growth of cargoism. The fertiliser has been blatant inequality; agitation for redress has been the natural fruit. In Papua New Guinea, this agitation has been cargoist in form; only as education has spread has it worn more rational clothes.

Students and their parents sought education as a means to an end, not as the end itself. The end was not possessions, it was equality with, and the respect of, the white man. This is the transmutation that education could bring about. The 'could' is Alkan Tololo's, Minister of Education in the late 1970's: 'The sense of insecurity, which is the basic cause of . . . cargo cult thinking, could disappear with the spread of education.'[67] The Minister was by no means certain that it would disappear. He knew that because its roots went deep, cargoism would die hard.

References

[1]Worsley (1970), p. 128.
[2]Mileng, Stahl in Steinbauer (1974), p. 177.
[3]Worsley (1970), p. 223.
[4]Kiki (1968), pp. 55, 60.
[5]Eri (1973), p. 131.
[6]Somare, Michael, 'In a Japanese school' in Beier (1974), pp. 72–4; Somare (1975), p. 3.
[7]Lawrence (1964), p. 105.
[8]Oliver (1973), p. 128.
[9]Oram (1976), p. 67.
[10]Ruhen (1963), p. 196.
[11]Nelson (1974), p. 82.
[12]Rowley (1965), p. 168.

[13]Wendt, Albert, *Pouliuli*, Auckland, Longman, Paul Ltd. (1977), pp. 55, 56.

[14]Worsley (1970), p. 196.

[15]Oram (1976), p. 81.

[16]White (1965), p. 130.

[17]Nelson (1974), p. 86.

[18]Hogbin (1951), p. 13.

[19]Worsley (1970), p. 135.

[20]Souter (1963), p. 238.

[21]'Second Reading Speech of the Hon. E. J. Ward, Minister for External Territories on the Papua–New Guinea Provisional Administration Act 1945', Canberra, Typescript, pp. 2, 5–6, in Jinks *et al.* (1973), p. 322.

[22]Ike, Chukwuemeka, *The Potter's Wheel*, Glasgow, Collins (Fontana) (1974), pp. 37–9.

[23]Munonye, John, *Obi*, London, Heinemann Educational Books (1969), pp. 123–6.

[24]Eri (1973), pp. 143–4.

[25]Finney (1973), p. 139; Strelan (1977), p. 32.

[26]Worsley (1970), p. 197.

[27]ibid.

[28]Lawrence (1964), p. 123.

[29]McCarthy (1963), pp. 224, 225.

[30]Morauta (1974), pp. 38, 39.

[31]ibid.

[32]Brown, Paula, 'Social change and social movements' in Fisk (1966), p. 155.

[33]Souter (1963), p. 241.

[34]Lawrence (1964), p. 124.

[35]ibid., p. 225.

[36]Eri (1973), pp. 140, 168.

[37]Wolfers (1975), p. 122.

[38]Matane (1972), pp. 84, 85.

[39]Fisk, E. K. & Tait, Maree, 'Aid' in Hudson (1975), p. 107.

[40]Burridge (1969), p. 65.

[41]Eri (1973), p. 46.

[42]Lawrence (1964), pp. 169, 170.

[43]Nzekwu, Onuora, *Blade Among the Boys*, London, Heinemann Educational Books (1972), p. 86.

[44]Threlfall (1975), p. 153.

[45]Tomkins & Hughes (1969), p. 59.

[46]'Cargo cult threats to teachers', *PNG Post-Courier* 6/75, in Weeks (1976), p. 35.

[47]Matane (1972), p. 103.

[48]McCarthy (1963), p. 181.

[49]Ruhen (1963), p. 199.

[50]Brown, Paula, 'Social change and social movements' in Fisk (1966),

p. 163; Hallpike (1977), p. 26; Smith (1975), p. 6; and Ruhen (1963), p. 202.

[51] Strelan (1977), p. 48.

[52] Finney (1973), p. 40.

[53] ibid., pp. 49, 51.

[54] ibid., pp. 80, 81.

[55] Orken, M. B., 'They fight for fun' in Sack (1974), p. 143.

[56] Rowley (1965), p. 183.

[57] Lawrence (1964), pp. 136, 150; McCarthey (1963), p. 226.

[58] Strelan (1977), p. 47.

[59] ibid., p. 43.

[60] Ruhen (1963), p. 210.

[61] Stent (1977), p. 191.

[62] Brown, Paula, 'Social change and social movements' in Fisk (1966), p. 157.

[63] Epstein (1969), p. 290.

[64] Clarke (1975), pp. 148, 374.

[65] Strelan (1977), p. 11.

[66] Kaspou, Bernard, in Weeks (1977), p. 109.

[67] Tololo, Alkan, 'A consideration of some likely future trends in education in PNG' in Thomas (1976), p. 221.

4

A land held in trust

The expeditions of Rowlands and Levien in the 1920s, and of the Leahy brothers, Dwyer, and Jim Taylor in the 1930s, had begun the long process of opening up the Highlands. Kainantu, the first government station to be established in the Highlands, was the base from which most patrols set out. Then the war preoccupied all who might have sought out souls, or gold, or taxpayers in more peaceable times, and the people of the Highlands were left to mind their own business as before. Very few had seen the white men; many had seen and heard their planes; and some even saw the casual strafing of administration and mission buildings about Kainantu, by aircraft said to be Japanese.[1] With the end of the war, patrols increased in number and penetration. Jim Taylor introduced money to the people of the Goroka district in 1947, and Ian Downs invited them to coffee. Now that there was money in circulation, and a means of making it, it only needed Leahy's trade store (to be followed by branches of the Steamships and Burns Philp chains) for there to be an opportunity to spend it.[2] There was the airstrip, there came a bank, an hotel, a church or two and a post office; and there came more white men, women and children, and they built themselves houses of permanent materials in neat lines. They bought land, settled on it, planted it, and profited. The locals profited, too; but like the people of the Chimbu, the people of the Asaro valley discovered the hard way that it took time to accumulate money enough to buy the tenth part of what the whites bought daily. The Chimbu began to sell their coffee in 1958, and for a while they had money to spend. But it was not long before they realised that the rate at which they could process coffee beans by hand set limits to their productivity. This in turn set limits to the amount of money that they could accumulate, and to the sort of goods that they could hope to buy. This realisation, as Brown says, induced feelings of helplessness and despondency in men only recently (and barely) pacified by promises.[3]

I have said (in Chapter Two) that the native had three patrons: the missions, the entrepreneurs, and the civil authorities. The first sought to educate the natives in their own community context, schooling a sufficient number of them to act as a catalyst in their families and villages. The second sought to train natives to be competent clerks, storemen, technicians and interpreters. Tomkins and Hughes call the period 1947–51, in which the latter philosophy was in the ascendancy, 'years of intensive exploitation'.[4] The administration did not involve itself in education in a positive way at this time, for fear that it would tread on the toes of one or other of its co-patrons. Tomkins and Hughes (missionaries themselves) convict the entrepreneurs of advancing blacks in their own interest; the churches, they say, had a clearer idea of the people's real needs and, to judge by the increasing emphasis on community education in the 1970s, the government came to agree with them. Ironically, however, it was the entrepreneurs who met the people's real wants. It may have been in the interest of the planters, store managers, and shop owners that the schools should turn out youths fit for employment; but parents and pupils supposed that this was in their interest, too. They wanted nothing better than to enter the modern sector of the economy, to be wage earners, to work for white men, and leave the village. It was not only in Papua New Guinea that the consumers resisted missionary attempts – as they saw it – to keep them in their place. In fairness to the missions, however, it might be said that if they had set their sights higher, they could not have guaranteed correspondingly higher level employment, even to their most successful pupils. They were caught between popular expectation of the good life, as exemplified by the whites, and the unwillingness of the whites to gratify this expectation – at least in the term defined by the white expatriate (like Ian Smith of Rhodesia) as his 'lifetime'. When at their best the missionaries gave their pupils a Christian model of behaviour – one consistent with 'development' in any context, at any level – their teaching was subverted by the model of acquisitive behaviour offered by arriviste Europeans.

The government first played a part in education, in any systematic way, as from August 1945. It was in this month that W. C. Groves was appointed Director of Education for the whole territory of Papua and New Guinea.[5] Groves had already shown his hand, ten years before, when he had declared his faith in: 'the possibility and value of devising an education which will belong truly to New Guinea: an education which will be bound up with the people's past and which will provide for their future progress in directions that will not bring the native into competition or rivalry with the Europeans.'[6] Percy Chatterton – in spite of this expression of an opinion with which he cannot have agreed – commended Groves for his 'enlightened guidance' of the education system, after 1946.[7] It is possible that the war caused Groves to repent his earlier view – it did give pause to paternalism in many an old colonial – for Chatterton looked forward with optimism, in the immediate post-war years, to the building of a system on the foundations laid by the missions; to the policy, that is, of Administrator Griffiths before 1935. Chatterton would not have held the native in as low esteem as Groves.

Much of the money disbursed by the Australian administration in 'war damage' payments, may have been spent by native recipients on 'manufactured' goods at inflated prices, as Burridge claims;[8] but the payments were not always in cash. The government school at Maprik, established in 1949, was in compensation for war damage. And such a foundation could have a pump-priming effect, as evidenced by the building of Catholic and Protestant Mission Schools in the district soon thereafter.[9] Still, this was small beer when we consider the extent of the need: more than ninety-five per cent of the population of two million was illiterate in the late 1940s; there were fewer than 5,000 graduates of the primary schools, only twenty-seven high-school graduates, and not one single exceptional university graduate, on whom hopes for the future might rest.[10] Three new, or restored, schools in Maprik would not go far to redeem a state as sorry as this.

What is almost more lamentable is that the authorities did not help those natives enterprising enough to want to help themselves. John Teosin and Francis Hagai were at mission elementary schools on Buka Island, in the early 1950s. They discontinued their studies, and returned to their home village determined to put what they had learnt to some practical effect. In Hagai's words: 'We held a meeting of all our relatives, and suggested that instead of working separately, we should all work together. Thirty people were ready to try and we started in a small way . . . We put all our fowls together, instead of keeping them in separate runs, and we grew some peanuts, which we sold to traders. Soon people saw that our idea was a good one, and they joined us.'[11] By the mid-1960s, half the island was involved in one way or another in the activities of what was by now the Hahalis Welfare Society, an officially registered private company. These activities included the production of copra and dried cocoa beans, the maintenance of eight co-operative stores, the running of trucks, even the building of feeder roads.

Community development was in the air: army officers had talked about it; teachers were given to teaching, and missionaries to preaching about it; experts from Australia and the United States recommended it; research was conducted into it, books written about it, and reports filed. It was an idea whose time had come in ex-colonies the world over. In V. S. Naipaul's novel *A House for Mr Biswas*,[12] a welfare officer enthuses about the potential for co-operative ventures of all sorts, in Trinidad. In Bessie Head's Botswana (*When Rain Clouds Gather*)[13] a European agronomist persuades villagers to abandon destructive cattle herding, and turn to cash cropping, fencing, controlled irrigation, and co-operative farming. And in Sebukima's Uganda (*A Son of Kabira*) a young African counterpart of John Teosin persuades the big men of his village to pool their resources and establish a co-operative.[14]

All might have been well at Hahalis, if the society had not attracted to itself the animosity of the local Marist Mission. Certain of the activities of the society may have had a cargoist tint; its leaders may even have encouraged bigger land-owners to dream, in order to win their support for the society's straight economic programme. For his part, Albert Kiki – on a fact-finding tour – was satisfied that the 'rumours that spoke of some evil religion practised at Hahalis' were baseless.[15] They had more to do with mission pique than with evidence of the gross immorality with which Teosin and Hagai were charged. The Welfare Society had virtually established a church of its own. This is not surprising given that it had established so much else of its own, and that one new denomination or another, each calling itself the true church of God, was raising its cross on the New Guinea Islands with every new moon. The civil authorities did not take mission complaints too seriously. What it did take exception to was that in January 1962, the Society's leaders persuaded its members to refuse to pay the annual head tax.

In the normal course, the administration was keen to encourage the growth of co-operative societies. Before the war, those that were established had to be compelled into being. During the war, co-operation was all the talk in the Papuan Infantry Battalion, and in the labour lines; Japanese and allied wealth sowed seeds that sprang up in all sorts of wonderful ways in 1945. Societies grew spontaneously under colourful leaders, with high-reaching plans. The official view of these developments was expressed by Mr (later Sir) Percy Spender, Minister for External Territories, in 1950. In distant Canberra, he wrote:

> The co-operative movement has been introduced into the Territory and the Administration is guiding and sponsoring natives in the formation of societies under this movement. The natives have displayed a keenness to participate in the movement which is being encouraged by the Administration as it affords a splendid opportunity to the native for self help and as a practical means of education in the ways of modern society.[16]

Put like this, the movement appears to have been carefully cultivated; all was under control and according to plan. J. D. Legge's impression is that the movement was *sui generis*, that it burst forth independently of official efforts, and threatened to grow, and fruit on its own, luxuriantly beyond management.[17] White businessmen deplored the growth of so many societies; private shipping firms refused to carry cargo from New South Wales to the co-operatives on the New Guinea coast, for example.[18] But this sort of action was not sanctioned by the authorities, any more than they gave ear to mission accusations of irreligion. Individual patrol officers, or their agents, might have upset the tables of the money-changers on occasion, and stamped on their flowers; there is no accounting for the panic reactions of the few at the outposts of empire.[19] On the whole, the administration was happy to guide the growth of the societies, as Spender claimed – especially where they might have the positive effect, for example of supplying Port Moresby with fresh fruit and vegetables. But that the Tommy Kabu movement in the Purari Delta was unable to market cash crops in sufficient quantity either to satisfy consumer demand, or to realise an income that would gratify members' expectations, was the primary cause of its downfall. A secondary cause (and a flaw in the workings of all such native-led societies) was its indifferent accounting. What too many government officials were quick to call cupidity, or embezzlement, was really no more than simple incompetence. More than one 'Kompani sekateri' went to prison because he did not obey the four rules of arithmetic.

Co-operative farming, then, was not an idea that the administration had to work hard to 'sell' to peasant farmers, clan-conscious as they were, or schooled of a sudden by the war. They were as ready for community development schemes in the 1940's and 1950's, as they had been for baptism a generation before. What the evangelists in both cases failed to take into account was that their gospels would be assimilated to mechanistic, materialistic – not to say simplistic – views of the world and its working. Fundamental to these views was adherence to the principle of compensation: goods were given, in order that goods should be received; the spirits had been kept happy, with a view to a happy return; European means would be adopted to ensure European ends. Whether or not the villagers understood community development, co-operative farming, and corporate welfare as cargoism made modern, they certainly looked to the 'movement' to confer benefits in cash and kind – benefits commensurate with their investment of land, labour and zeal.

Their hopes of the local government councils were of the same kind. Missionaries had allowed converts to believe in this-worldly salvation, in the efficacy of prayer, faith, offertory payments and Bible reading in the here and now. Community development officers had allowed society members to believe that they would earn a cash income from the sale of farm produce, without first making sure that there would be a ready market for it, and that those responsible for managing the society's books had an

elementary understanding of figures.[20] In their turn, the administration officials who descended on villages to preach local taxes and
councils, expected rather more of their audiences than was wise.
They appeared to think that councils would distract the villagers
from the cults; that representation and discussion would take the
place of ritual and confusion. Instead, what often happened was
that the villagers understood taxation, and council meeting in new-
fashioned cargoist terms. This is not surprising when we consider
some of the (yet more) promises that were made. The Nasioi of
Bougainville had become disaffected; officials projected that a
council would mop up the enthusiasm being dissipated in cult
activity, and regain the people for sane self-help. Consequently,
says Oliver:

> a great proportion of the patrol officer's time and energy went in 'sales'
> talks' for the council. Nasioi proponents of the council . . . became
> sufficiently enthusiastic to exaggerate further the already grandiose
> administration claims of what a council would accomplish. The
> favourite theme . . . was 'If we have a council we will live like
> Europeans'. The patent absurdity of some of these claims provided fuel
> for the anti-council majority.[21]

African fiction supplies some interesting parallels. The Nigerian
novelist, T. M. Aluko, for example, describes a local government
council meeting in *His Worshipful Majesty*. The members are
debating their development priorities. It is generally agreed that
education is top of the list, but there is some doubt as to whether
hospitals or a modern water supply should come next. Ideas for
telephones and television are aired, until it is pointed out that these
are concerns of the central government.[22] It is unlikely that John
Teosin and Francis Hagai were so ingenuous as to hope that
revenue from the poll tax would return to them in the form of
telephones and television, but it is certain that they expected
tangible returns of some sort. The compensation principle might
have been supposed to operate with force when what was given
was shillings and pence. Cash had purchasing power no matter
whose purse it came from. But no roads, no government schools,
no aid-posts were built, so in 1962, the poll tax was withheld.
There were clashes, the administration took punitive action,
hundreds were sentenced to gaol, and feelings ran high. But John

Teosin engaged a lawyer canny enough to make hay of the kiap's legal powers; so the detainees were released once again. When calm was restored, the administration constructed a good all-weather road running the length of the island, so as to facilitate the transport of cash crops and trade goods.[23] John Teosin continued to enjoy the respect of the islanders, to amass a considerable fortune, and to be untouchable. What is more, Buka continued to withhold tax payments until well after independence day.[24]

There had been little in the way of educational planning before the war, as we have seen. The stated policy of the administration in the 1950's was to proceed to universal primary education by 1975.[25] It was the view of the then Minister for Territories, Paul (later Sir Paul) Hasluck, that the British had been too hasty in their withdrawal from Africa; they had educated a native élite at Achimota (Ghana), and Siriana (Kenya), had skimmed the milk at Fourah Bay and Makerere, and whipped the cream at Oxbridge and London – then, having created this anti-colonial élite, they had had to leave in a hail of brickbats. Hasluck had no intention of repeating this 'mistake'. Accordingly, he tried to secure uniform development, whereby all regions would advance at the same rate. He took this policy even to the extent of calling upon 'more advanced people' to hold back while more backward areas caught up.[26] More particularly, his objectives have been summarised as follows:

(1) To achieve mass literacy, that is to say, to attempt to teach all native children to read and write in a common language;
(2) To show them the way, awaken their interest in, and assist their progress towards . . . a civilised mode of life;
(3) To teach them what is necessary to them . . . to sustain a higher material standard of living . . .
(4) To retain what is best in native life and to blend it with the influences of western civilisation . . .
(5) To replace paganism by the acceptance of the Christian faith and the ritual of primitive life by the practice of religion.[27]

These were by no means illiberal objectives. Indeed, they were perhaps the only realistic objectives that could have been set at that time, in that place. They were priorities (says Geoffrey Smith) fully in line with 'the views that were then widely held about educational policy in developing countries'.[28] We are all given to wisdom after

the event, especially when that event has been superseded by so
many others. Hasluck is reproached now with having been of the
old school – a colonial thinker set in colonial ways. It is as well,
therefore, to listen to a modern Australian judgement on him (by
Ryan,[29] editor of the *Encyclopaedia of Papua New Guinea*), before
sentence is passed: 'Hasluck unfortunately is very old-fashioned,
and has an unhappy knack of not being believed or taken seriously
by many younger writers . . . But the fact is that he was the most
'serious' colonial thinker we ever had, and he *worked at it* in a way
quite unknown hitherto in this country.' It was the bit about the
'higher material standard of living', referred to in the third of the
above objectives, that the natives liked best. If education would
secure this for them they were all for it. They had no more interest
at present in the 'creation of a narrow educated elite'[30] than Hasluck
himself. One of my Grade 10 students, Kaiyuwento Yabuoh, gave
me this account of the popular expectation:

> When school first came to my village, the older people believed that
> when they put their children in school, they will get the white man's
> knowledge and will contact our dead relatives and bring goods to our
> village. Others believed that their children will bring wealth when they
> finish school and find jobs. Those who put their children into school
> boasted that they will be wealthy and others who heard the boasting of
> them brought their children into the school, too.

Another student, Joseph Waunuhoc, tells the same story:

> When the whites came and settled they started to build many new
> schools. They told the people that they all must go to school and get
> some education and get to know about new things and new ways of
> living. These whites told the people that if they all go to school and get
> good education and complete a certain stage, then you will all be like us.
> You will earn more money and you will be very rich. So the first people
> believed these Europeans and they all attended schools.

It hardly matters whether or not European settlers really did make
such outlandish promises for six years of primary schooling; what
does matter is that the natives understood what was said, in terms
of being 'very rich' and having 'plenty of things'. Education was
over-sold, in the same way as Christianity, and community
development, had been over-sold. The market ambition of the

Europeans was that education would take the place of cargo practice in the people's affections – that the new products would change consumer habits; yet the sales talk was pitched (necessarily) at the same level of understanding, with the result that the new product was sought after, and bought, as if it was merely a much improved version of the old one. The above students were Eastern Highlanders for whom schools of any sort were still something of a novelty. That their doors were now to be opened wider than before was good news indeed. These were the students for whom 'more advanced people' were being asked to wait, before demanding the secondary, and tertiary, education that they might have considered their due.

One attraction of the new policy (of higher subsidies to mission schools, for example), to the people of 'more sophisticated districts', was that the 'common language' of the schools, and of the 'mass literacy', was to be English. The coastals and islanders – schooled, as like as not, in the vernacular, or Pidgin, or Motu – could afford to wait if in the meantime they could learn the language of their masters.

In the early 1950s, the government was undecided as to what should be the language of instruction in schools. There were three points of view, held and expressed by one group or another: there were those who felt that the mother tongue, or lingua franca, should be the language of instruction throughout the primary course, with English taught as one subject among many; there were those who felt national unity would demand a common tongue, but that this should be introduced as the language of instruction only after the second or third year of primary schooling; and there were those who argued for the use of English as the medium of instruction from the very beginning of the course. Chatterton was a spokesman for the first view. He advocated use of the mother tongue, so that the school should not be 'divorced from the community'.[31] The U.N. Trusteeship Council, on the other hand, would not countenance the use of Pidgin at any level, and recommended its 'eradication from the Teritory altogether'.[32] Hasluck's policy, it has been said, was to establish a universal primary schooling that would underpin formal institutions of a democratic society. European culture was taken to be the model to which 'what is best in native life' would be assimilated. Thus it was decided that the only fit medium for the transmission of 'a civilised mode of life' was English. Those whom White calls 'the idealists, who heatedly damned Pidgin as undignified, inadequate and degraded',[33] and whom Chatterton vilifies as 'linguistic cargo-cultists', won over the government, if not all the governed. Those who did not go to school, and many of those who did, picked up Pidgin regardless of the refined distaste of expatriates.

Chatterton was the exception rather than the rule among missionary teachers, where the English language teaching policy was concerned. There was little room in the 1950s for schools that held out against government subsidies, and therefore government directives (especially after 1952, when the administration began 'recognising' schools, and registering them). More schools were wanted, schools of a higher standard than before. There were no indigenous teachers to staff these new schools, and no more than the longest serving white missionaries spoke a local tongue or two. Volunteer teachers from abroad, contract teachers from 'down south', education officers, textbook writers – all spoke English, and expected other people to do the same. Nelson Giraure describes how he was considered bright enough after some years at his mission school, to proceed to a government school. Because the medium of instruction at this school was English, young Nelson had to start all over again in Class 1. There were large signs on the walls all over the school bearing the words: 'You must speak English only'. Children caught breaking this rule, he says, were 'punished with grass-cutting, extra work, or smacks'.[34] Another student, Benjes Alusi from Western Province, remembers 'two or three canes across the bottom, and an hour's grass-cutting' for the same offence; 'any slip of the tongue would have your name on the punishment list' adds a third – Kare Dumba of Madang.[35] Pidgin and the vernacular were both outlawed from start to finish of the school day, even at boarding schools.

Even if the missions had attempted to resist the drive to 'mass literacy' in English, it is far from certain that parents would have continued to enrol children at their schools. But the missions did not make the attempt, at least, not in any concerted way. On the contrary, the Australian Board of Missions, in 1956, affirmed quite concertedly, that: 'English is the only possible solution to the unity of New Guinea, and unity there must be as the people grow into a nation'.[36] The affirmation was something of a compromise, however, in that the Board was convinced that children would make most progress in English if they were taught to read and write their own language first. This was also the view, it may be said, of the 1951 Platten survey for UNESCO, and of linguisticians of some renown. Platten contended that fluency in English was best achieved by teaching it as a subject from the first year, and using it as the medium of instruction only after some two or three years' use of the mother tongue, or of a lingua franca, already understood and spoken. It looked for a time as if the administration would heed the advice of this survey, since it commissioned a number of school books in certain of the more commonly spoken vernaculars, including Kuanua.[37] One of the above linguisticians, S. A. Wurm, argued for use of the mother tongue in the first years, in the interests of 'proficiency and speed of basic education'; he made light of the shortage of textbooks in the vernaculars, and of qualified teachers who spoke them[38] – but by the mid-1950s, these and hardening attitudes in Canberra, were the rocks on which his argument foundered. It was a strong argument, but the rocks were stronger still.

The administration gave the native peoples what it thought they wanted. The way from elementary to secondary schooling was a 'narrow path' in Papua New Guinea, as it was in Ghana. In his autobiographical novel of this name, Selormey describes the sequence of examinations that had blocked his path, up to the final rite of passage, the School Leaving Certificate.[39] Naipaul refers to the similar trials in the way of Elias, a would-be doctor in Port of Spain. In the Trinidad of the 1940s, the only means by which one could realise such an aim was via the Cambridge Senior School Certificate, and a boat ticket to England.[40] In Papua New Guinea, a generation later, the path was still narrower. The administration, in 1954, began awarding twenty scholarships annually to particularly promising native students, to allow them to attend secondary schools in Australia.[41] At the same time, what Oram calls 'true secondary education', began when selected students at Sogeri, near Port Moresby, embarked on a Queensland secondary education course, by correspondence.[42] They were tentative beginnings, but they were enough to have a backwash effect on the primary schools. Thanks to the centralisation of control since 1952 – the registration of schools, and the certification of teachers – standards were rising. The introduction of post-primary classes in certain government schools (particularly the urban schools), and the possibility of selection for 'true secondary education', sharpened the focus of teaching in the upper-primary grades, on school-leaving examinations.[43] What is more, teaching in English was set at a still higher premium than before. In spite of Hasluck's egalitarian education policy, and his faith in the sufficiency of elementary schooling, parents began to see the first school merely as the preparation for the second. No one had suggested that any other language than English was appropriate for the secondary level; if, to reach this level, one had to have a good grounding in English, then the sooner English was used as the medium of instruction in primary schools, the better.

In 1940, there had been 90,000 children attending territory primary schools.[44] Twenty years later, Hasluck could make a boast of the following figures: '. . . today there are over 400 European teachers and some 5,400 native teachers at work in 4,100 schools attended by 196,000 pupils.'[45]

As the PNG population increased in size – medicine was bound to have a dramatic effect, in a country where public health had been so neglected – and as the cost of providing formal education rose, so the target of 100 per cent primary schooling by 1975 looked increasingly unattainable. Hasluck's hoped-for 'uniform development' might have worked well enough if time had permitted, if the United Nations Organization had not been looking over the government's shoulder, and if, what Spate calls, the 'political sector' had not forged ahead with a momentum of its own.[46] As it was, colonies in Africa set a faster pace. Macmillan's 'wind of change' was felt even in the Pacific. Sogeri graduates were beginning to ask questions about their country's future, and ministers were having to find answers that placed more responsibility for that future in native hands. The size of the public service in PNG was doubled in the five years 1953–8; yet such was the turnover among expatriate public servants, and so many were the posts to be filled at a time of rapid expansion, that the numbers of officers always fell far short of full strength in all departments.[47] The time could not long be delayed before these places would be filled with native graduates of a complete cycle of secondary education. All that were needed were the graduates, the schools, the teachers, the textbooks, the finance, and the will.

There was no hiding the opportunities for advancement, from the would-be graduates themselves. The pupils were on the starting-blocks already, and their parents were standing right behind them, waiting for the gun. They wanted education, and they wanted it in English. Like Vambe's young Rhodesians, they were 'more than willing to be sucked into the materialistic machine of the white man. In fact they hurled themselves into the new order with . . . enthusiasm.'[48] The accounts of my own students of their (fathers' and uncles') recollections of the coming of the schools are full of the realisation of the importance of the white man's language. Afaya Pu'uo writes: 'When their children speak English their parents thought they are speaking birds' language. Then two or three years pass by, their children get good jobs and have good pay and their parents realise the way of western people.' Mainia Ta'o's father was the first in his village to know Pidgin, and to 'walk with the white man'. The whites 'told him about education', Mainia writes: 'First, when he heard of it, he had no idea of it, but later he saw natives walking with whites. Those knew a bit about read and write they earn high pay, among the other natives. So he realised it and said to himself, let me send my son to school.' Hagameyo Mokupe puts it in a nutshell:

> People of my village were happy because their children are in school to learn Whiteman's language, the only idea they had. Subsequently, people realised that after completing school, their children (would) work for money. From then onwards people of my village regard school as an important place to learn Whiteman's language before getting jobs.

Without doubt, pupils and parents regarded acquisition of literacy in English as their greatest asset. Asked why he wanted to learn to read, one canny Highlander explained that he would like to be able to check the coffee buyer's scales.[49] Undoubtedly, there was an element of wrong-headed prestige seeking in the popular demand for English language learning. Like Balinde, in Tanzania, who looked forward to learning English for the status that it would confer on him, and for the opportunity that the use of 'long words' would give him to 'flabbergast' his companions,[50] so there must have been many a New Guinean whose dreams were superficial and egocentric. Then again, there were many who had cause to value literacy in English. The three students quoted above were all in Grade 10, with high hopes of securing wage-employment, or places on Grade 11 courses in national high schools. They had reason to think that their proficiency in English would stand them in good stead, in what we are pleased to call 'the real world'. But there is a good deal of evidence that school leavers who returned to their villages, 'failures' in the eyes of their schools and villagers, continued to value the English that they had learnt. Wilson led a university research team in the Western Highlands, in 1972, with a brief to interview school-leavers like these. He found that of forty-nine ex-students, all but one considered English language teaching to be the single most important job done by the schools – and their parents agreed with this judgement.[51] Six years later, a very similar investigation drew very similar conclusions. Though school-leavers considered that they could have put their knowledge of English to more obvious use in urban employment, those who returned to the village claimed to be regular readers of English translations of the Bible, and of Australian comics.[52] The knowledge of English continued to be 'useful' to them.

It is an irony that has beset education planners in almost all the 'less developed countries', that the knowledge that they perceive to be most useful, is set at a discount by its consumers. Some doubt has been cast on the ability of school-leavers to speak and write English to an acceptable standard – particularly as native teachers have replaced expatriates[53] – but on the whole, the place of English in the curriculum has not been in dispute. It is both a high status and an applied subject, that rare bird of paradise, a combination of the 'academic' and the 'vocational'. Agriculture is not such a bird; and nor are technical studies. Planners all over French and English-speaking Africa have first established (or adopted) grammar schools on the metropolitan model, and then have set up schools for the non-élite. Technical and rural studies were to be on the curriculum since it was supposed that the products of these latter schools would be the informed farmers and technicians of the future. It was not long before parents and public compared the jobs and salaries that went to the graduates of the 'academic' schools, with those that went to the graduates of the 'vocational' schools. It was a matter for chagrin – but it should not have been a matter for surprise – among planners, that the 'vocational' schools were judged to be inferior, and that in consequence they were unpopular. The novelist Camara Laye spoke for Guinea when he put these words into the mouth of Konate, a teacher: 'Everybody wants to be a clerk! Doubtless it's fairly natural that youthful ambition should manifest itself in that way and that it should tend to the pen-pushing occupations, despite the demands of industry for technicians, and of commerce for skilled workers. It's very disheartening that technicians are not taken seriously.'[54] And Sivi, a highlander, spoke for New Guinea, when he told Director of Education Roscoe, in 1959: 'we want our children to be exactly like you'.[55] Sivi spoke for all those parents who rejected 'relevant' education with a 'rural bias'. In 1973, fourteen 'skulankas' ('school-anchors') were set up, designed to teach practical skills to Grade 6 school-leavers. Stress was laid on 'community involvement', but the community was not impressed by a two-year, terminal training for the rejected. In consequence, within only five years, nine of the skulankas had closed down, and the five that remained had been reorganised as 'vocational centres' for students at Grade nine.[56]

In some areas, schools designed for pupils who would return to work clan land had come too late. The vocational school at Vunamami on the Gazelle Peninsula was one such. It failed not merely because parents objected to what they understood to be a 'deliberate attempt to retard their children's progress in education',[57] but because there was too little clan land left for the pupils to return to. The three-and-a-half acres per head that had been available in 1875, had been reduced to two-thirds of an acre by 1961.[58] For this reason, the Tolai of that district had little choice but to seek wage-earning employment to which only a regular high-school certificate would grant access. Education with a 'rural bias' was still less relevant to their needs in the modern sector of the economy, than having to learn Tennyson's 'Half a League, half a league' and Byron's 'The Destruction of Sennacherib's Host' would have been. Epstein recounts a dispute between two descent-groups on Matupit Island, over land leased by the administration for the building of a European teacher's house.[59] Land was just as big an issue in East New Britain (as well as in Port Moresby), as in Ngugi's Kenya, and in the New Zealand of the Maori novelist,

Patricia Grace. The attitude towards the land among the Papuans of Port Moresby – who have realised too late how cheaply their fathers sold clan lands for short term gain – is very little different from that of the Maoris of North Island, with their respect for what Grace calls the 'Tapu places' in the hills.[60]

It was the report of the UN visiting mission of 1962 (sometimes called the Foot Report, after Sir Hugh Foot, its principal), that discredited the Hasluck policy of uniform development and gradualism. The policy was brusquely overturned in ringing calls for expansion of facilities for secondary education, and for an immediate start to plans for an indigenous university. Of the 205,833 pupils in school in 1961, no fewer than 198,930 (or ninety-seven per cent of the total) were in primary schools.[61] The demand for secondary schooling was clamant; and it would soon be irresistible. The Commission stated the case as follows: 'The need for qualified personnel in all fields is so great and so urgent that a new approach is essential. The mission believes that the Administration should be planning now to provide an annual turn-out of university graduates of the order of at least a hundred.'[62]

This was a modest enough programme, yet by the time Gough Whitlam made his tour of the territory in 1972, there was still only one qualified, indigenous lawyer, and there were no fully qualified doctors, dentists, architects, or surveyors, and no native executives in commercial companies at all.[63] Even at the lowest levels of the public service, the target was only one third native officers by 1967. The work that lay ahead – the planning, the money-raising, the building, the equipping, the teacher-training – was formidable indeed. The amount by which, and the rate at which, the system would need to grow were food for the thought of a novelist (in the Nigerian elementary school context):

'At thirty-five kids to a class and six classes per school you have two hundred and ten per school. Say two hundred, allowing for five per cent wastage. That gives how many schools?' . . .
'Seven thousand, five hundred schools. The 1952 census showed eight hundred and forty seven' elementary schools already existing in the country. Eleven per cent of the requirement. Eighty-seven per cent of these are owned and run by the missions . . .
'The Director of Public Works tells us that each school can be expected

to cost £3,000. On your building programme alone you require . . .'
Shepherd looked at George for the answer.
'Eighteen million pounds!' George did the sum.[64]

Doing the sums was one thing; a novelist could do the sums. What
was to be done with the answers was another matter altogether.

References

[1]Sinclair (1971), p. 42.
[2]Finney (1973), p. 37.
[3]Brown (1973), pp. 122, 123.
[4]Tomkins & Hughes (1969), pp. 81, 82.
[5]Louisson (1974), p. 12.
[6]quoted in Smith (1975), p. 9.
[7]Chatterton (1974), p. 83.
[8]Burridge (1969), p. 66.
[9]Stent (1977), p. 205.
[10]Todd (1974), p. 113.
[11]quoted in Oliver (1973), pp. 150, 151.
[12]Naipual, V. S., *A House for Mr Biswas*, London, Collins (Fontana)
(1963), pp. 431, 432.
[13]Head, Bessie, *When Rain Clouds Gather*, London, Heinemann Educational Books (1972), pp. 37–40.
[14]Sebukima, Davis, *A Son of Kabira*, Nairobi, OUP (1969), pp. 99–103.
[15]Kiki (1968), p. 113.
[16]Spender, P. C., 'Australia's policy in relation to external territories' in
Jinks *et al* (1973), p. 341.
[17]Legge, J. D., 'Australian colonial policy' in ibid., p. 347.
[18]Tomkins & Hughes (1969), p. 103.
[19]Burridge (1960), p. 236; and Burridge (1969), p. 60.
[20]Oram (1976), p. 91.
[21]Oliver (1973), p. 149.
[22]Aluko, T. M., *His Worshipful Majesty*, London, Heinemann Educational Books (1973), pp. 20–1.
[23]Oliver (1973), p. 153.
[24]Williams, J., Headmaster of Buka High School, in a personal
communication, April 1978.
[25]Smyth (1976), p. 1.
[26]Oram, Nigel, 'Administration, development and public order' in
Clunies-Ross & Langmore (1973), p. 5.
[27]Essai (1961), p. 173.
[28]Smith (1975), p. 32.
[29]Ryan, Peter, in a personal communication, February 1984.

[30]Parker, R. S., 'The advance to responsible government' in Fisk (1968), p. 245.

[31]Chatterton (1974), p. 83.

[32]Essai (1961), p. 181.

[33]White (1965), p. 163.

[34]Giraure, Nelson, 'The need for a cultural programme: personal reflections' in Thomas (1976), p. 62.

[35]Weeks (1977), pp. 82, 124.

[36]Tomkins & Hughes (1969), p. 120.

[37]Threlfall (1975), p. 176.

[38]Wurm, S. A., 'Language and literacy' in Fisk (1968), pp. 137, 138.

[39]Selormey, Francis, *The Narrow Path*, London, Heinemann Educational Books (1967), pp. 180–2.

[40]Naipaul, V. S., *Miguel Street*, Harmondsworth, Penguin Books (1971), pp. 32–4.

[41]Parker, R. S., 'The Advance to responsible government' in Fisk (1968), p. 245.

[42]Oram (1976), p. 113.

[43]Louisson (1974), p. 114.

[44]Clarke (1975), p. 164.

[45]Hasluck, P. M. C., 'Australian policy in Papua and New Guinea' in Jinks *et al.* (1973), p. 362.

[46]Spate, O. H. N., 'Education and its problems' in Fisk (1968), p. 123.

[47]Parker, R. S., 'The growth of territory administration' in ibid., p. 207.

[48]Vambe, Lawrence, *An Ill-Fated People*, London, Heinemann Educational Books (1972), p. 198.

[49]Nelson (1974), p. 91.

[50]Ruhumbika, Gabriel, *Village in Uhuru*, London, Longman (1969), pp. 39–41.

[51]Wilson, Michael, 'School leavers in the village' in Powell & Wilson (1974), p. 133.

[52]Weeks (1978), pp. 73, 92.

[53]Lancy (1979), p. 94.

[54]Laye, Camara, *A Dream of Africa*, London, Collins (Fontana) (1970), p. 79.

[55]Smith (1975), p. 46.

[56]Conroy (1979), p. 104.

[57]Louisson (1974), p. 93.

[58]Smith (1975), p. 7.

[59]Epstein (1969), p. 283.

[60]Grace, Patricia, *Mutuwhenua: The Moon Sleeps*, Auckland, Longman Paul (1978), pp. 56–8.

[61]Souter (1963), p. 251.

[62]'Report of the 1962 UN Visiting Mission to the Trust Territory of New Guinea' in Jinks *et al.* (1973), p. 381.

[63]Oram (1976), p. 122.
[64]Aluko, T. M., *Chief the Honourable Minister*, London, Heinemann Education Books (1970), pp. 80–2.

5

Ripe for development

Before the Second World War, in Yam, children were sent to the Lutheran mission Central School in order to learn the cargo secret. When it became plain that the teachers were keeping it to themselves, one boy at least was taken away.[1] In the late 1940s, a Buka youth, John Teosin (later to be a founder member of the Hahalis Welfare Society) was sent to mission school in Rabaul, with a mission of his own: an older relative had instructed him to learn the 'mystical formula' for acquiring European wealth.[2] In the late 'seventies upper secondary school students could still speak in very similar terms about their parents' expectations of the return from investment in schooling. Aizo Avese had this to say:

> My relatives thought education was a key way to get money and be a rich man. They said: 'If you go to school, you will eat good food live in a good house and sit on a chair and just expect money in your pockets.' These types of ideas were brought up by the people who went for contract and worked as a labourer, and saw the clerks working in the business office and the typist sitting on the chair busy typing. They thought they were sitting on the chair doing nothing and only expecting money in their pockets. When they came home they put us in school and they expected us to sit on the chair and expect money to come in our pockets.

The magical element is never far below the surface of these expectations, though the expectations themselves were reasonable in the circumstances, and commonplace. Amukia Tendea reported as follows: 'My parents' opinion, or feelings towards the school, was that, if we go to school, we will change and become like the whites, in appearance and in character, such as wearing clean clothes, shoes, watches, forgetting the old customs and following the western customs, and to know much about the background of the whites . . .'

Richard Smith has written about the opening of a government primary school among the Wankung people, of the Upper Markham Valley, in 1962.[3] He outlined a 'logical paradigm', whereby the school was perceived as, first and foremost, the 'road' to European knowledge; the pupils must exploit their school knowledge to pass examinations and win jobs; money would automatically flow to the workers; and be used to compensate their parents and sponsors, for their outlay on school fees. (The parents might well be in debt to local big-men, acting as pay masters, in order to bind the parents to him as feudal warriors.[4]

We amuse ourselves debating whether this or that educational provision confers an investment or consumption good. The distinction is the staple of the literature of the economics of education. There was (and to a large extent, still is) no doubt in the minds of P.N.G. parents about which of these goods they look for: education was an investment, pure and simple. Smith's paradigm can be illustrated, time and again, in the testimony of students interviewed in the late 'seventies; but two or three examples will suffice. The above Amukia Tendea went on to say:

Another thing which they believed was that we will live in good houses like whites, and earn a good living where we can be rich and live western like, in huge buildings, with wide roads. They also believed that we would one day work and bring money to them, which they can buy their needs and wants.

When I first attended a community school, I was advised by my parents to behave and co-operate with students and teachers. I was told that once I got through schooling, I would have the knowledge which would enable me to get a really good job. Apart from that, they said they expected to get benefit from me after the long years of paying my school fees. (Topeni Reho)

they realised that education was a useful thing. They believed that if a child goes to school and gets a good education, he would get good jobs in government department, for a high salary. They realised that if their child works in any enterprises or government departments, they would get things free from them. I have experienced this with my own eyes. (Atatai Arabeba)

The paradigm is illustrated in research findings published by the Education Reseach Unit of the University of Papua New Guinea. A study in Mendi and Tari, in the Southern Highlands, revealed that pecuniary benefits were cited by fifty-three per cent of students asked why their parents wanted them to 'get as much education as possible';[5] and Joseph Waibu concluded from interviews with parents in Lumi, West Sepik, that they 'clearly associated education and knowledge with the idea that it would provide a source of material wealth . . . to the aged parents'.[6] Boys were sent to school before girls, because what their parents hoped for in their sons, they feared in their daughters. If the former left home and secured lucrative jobs, the necessity for further parental outlay was reduced – they might even be spared the expense of their sons' bride-price; but if their daughters left home, parents ran the risk of losing income from this same source. But if there was any money left after the boys' school fees had been paid, the girls would be next in the queue. Palmer intervewed girls at high school, and found that parents expected their daughters to undertake paid employment before marriage (but not after it), for only so long as it took to earn enough to repay school fees. 'Education was only seen as wasted,' writes Palmer 'if the girl did not repay fees'.[7] The investigations of Monson[8] and Stanton,[9] confirm the earlier findings of Conroy,[10] that a good rate of return was expected from investment in education.

Of course, there was nothing specifically Oceanic about this 'education-as-investment' syndrome; it can be illustrated by reference to novels from all over the British Empire. One example will suffice, from Eastern Nigeria, in which formal schooling is clearly identified with good business. A 'fat man' has saved up enough money to pay his son's school fees; his profit motive is as obvious as his oil-puncheon belly: 'He was a whiteman's cook, so he said. He had told everybody loudly that he had with his cooking, sent his son to college. His son would soon finish and join the Council and then money "like water-flow" he had said, rubbing his hands . . .'[11]

Government officers, and teachers preached the same message as the missionaries, and they sowed the seed of the same misapprehension. They cannot be held to account for the construction put upon unguarded words in unprepared speeches, by villagers whose vocabulary was small. But a promise is a promise. The kiaps who promised 'save, plenti moni, na hamamas' (knowledge, plenty of money, and happiness) after schooling, were believed no less implicitly than the army officers who promised a good time, after the war. It is worth quoting the kiap,[12] in the pidgin that he was obliged to use, for a flavour of the misunderstanding to which simple words could give rise:

> Taim yu salim pikinini igo sikul embai ikamap olsem mi whiteman. Em bai sikul na kisim big save, plenti moni, put shoe na soks olsem mi tru. Bihain bai yupela hamamas tru.
> When you send your children to school they'll become like the white man. At school they'll get much knowledge, and afterwards, plenty of money; they'll put shoes and socks on just like me. Then you'll all be very happy.

This note is struck frequently in non-fiction autobiography: Nelson Giraure writes of how he and his co-pupils were told over and over again that 'only the fools and the bush kanakas would return to the village.' Those with brains were destined for better things. They would 'get jobs and earn big money'. Giraure speaks of how his parents, and others, were similarly 'brainwashed'.[13] The Papua Besena (separatist) politician, Josephine Abaijah, wrote thus, of her desire for education: 'When I was at school, my teacher told me that when I became advanced and civilised like him, the Europeans would step aside and give me a chance in my own country.'[14] That was a promise the young Josephine would let no one forget.

Just as the building of new and better church buildings came to be the expression of old rivalries between the peoples of the Gazelle Peninsula,[15] so it came to be a matter of prestige to attract more expenditure from the authorities on mission aid posts, and schools, than the next village.[16] Smith wrote approvingly of the village of Panduaya, Mendi, whose people gave their labour voluntarily, and who supplied bush materials to build their own school rooms, and a house for the teacher.[17] What had been an isolated show of enterprise and enthusiasm, it was subsequently government policy to encourage. Many day high schools were built by their host communities, in the 1970s, since this was the only means by which schools could be provided in numbers sufficient to maintain a nation-wide ratio of Grade 6 leavers to Grade 7 entrants (of approximately three to one).[18] When the villagers did not build the school themselves (perhaps because it was to be a boarding school, of permanent materials), there were communities prepared to pay for the school buildings, rather than go without. Nelson tells of the Kol villagers of New Britain, who, when informed one day that they could have a vocational school if they helped pay for it, presented the authorities on the following day with a basket containing six thousand Australian dollars, and a promise of more if it was needed.[19] And when the competition for new schools was over, and the doors were open, a new competition began to see which of two village schools (in Manus, for example)[20] would be the first to be filled.

The building of the school, of course, was only the beginning. If it was a small bush primary school of woven pitpit and kunai grass, the expense was easily contained. Furniture came less cheaply; but the attendance fee was a recurrent expense that called for involvement in the cash economy, a certain thrift, and (it must be said) an uncommon capacity for long-term financial planning. The fee might not be large, but then neither was a villager's income. Kenneth Kaunda recalls his near failure to secure the education that made him Zambia's first president, for the want of two shillings and sixpence:

> There was no free universal education at that time and every parent had to find half a crown a year. Just before my father died, I had been ill with influenza and so unable to attend the opening of the school. When I did at last present myself at school the teacher asked for my two and sixpence, and when I told him that I had no money, he sent me back to my mother to get the necessary half-crown. I ran sobbing to her, but she had no money in the house and she wept with me. Fortunately, a kind neighbour came to our aid and lent us the money which was in due course repaid. For so small a thing in those days could a child for ever forfeit the privilege of his life's education.[21]

And for so small a thing, might Papua New Guinea have forfeited a Kenneth Kaunda or some mute inglorious Milton.

A school was one mark among many of modernisation. The community that stumped up the money for a school did the same when it came to investment in a more obviously money-making venture. Money was pooled for the purchase of a utility truck for the transport of coffee, trade goods, and/or paying passengers, or for the establishment of a trade store, or other 'bisnis'. But money-making was not necessarily the primary objective. Several writers testify to the prestige conferred on a village by the presence in it, of a trade store, be it ever so humble – indeed, as Finney writes, of the desire to own and operate commercial vehicles among the Gorokans,[22] prestige was no less 'investment-motive' than profit. The effort that had been expended in fighting now went into setting up stores, cattle projects, piggeries (and schools) – all that went under the name of 'develpman'.[23] Where profit was en-visaged, it was often expected to flow automatically from a simulacrum of economic activity: sitting at tables, exchanging goods for money, or the promise of money, and unpacking boxes, and writing on paper. That there was a trade store at all, on the white man's model, would ensure profits by sympathetic magic.[24] Few white men were surprised (but rather many were gratified) when the profits did not flow, and the trade store owners went bankrupt. Clarke refers to the 'frightening number of indigenous bankrupts' that were declared, so soon after the stores had been stocked, and business had begun.[25] The simple cause was ignorance of costs and returns. When status considerations were uppermost; when belief in the mystique of cargo was so durable (as it proved to be among Oliver's Bougainvilleans, for example);[26] and when shop owners sold goods to the family, and their friends, for less than they had paid, the shops emptied and were not re-filled. Similarly, when truck owners took their family and friends joy-riding in their new Toyota, Datsun, or Mitsubishi; when they drove a little recklessly, and the roads were bad, many new trucks were left in the ditch, or the creek, never to be started again. There were those Europeans who were entertained, there were those who were distressed, and there were those who said 'I told you so', but none should have been surprised.

It was fortunate that schools were maintained, and staffed, by missions and by government. These, at least, would not go bankrupt or rusty. But just as the prestige value of trade stores was reduced as they emptied, or, as time went on, they were run on business lines, and multiplied, so the prestige value of schools was reduced, when every village had one, and none was obviously superior to any other. Then the expectation was that they would deliver jobs; if they failed to do this, villagers lost interest in them. A high school student, Okima Avasi, told this story:

> . . . When the missionary first introduced the schooling system, he told them that they were going to gain some 'save'. That was the only word he mentioned to them . . .
>
> After so long of schooling, my uncle left school and walked all the way to Kainantu where he found himself a job. He worked for some months and with the money he earned, bought some clothes and walked back home.
>
> When he got home with those things, the people thought by going to school and gaining 'save', they would get a job and earn money to buy those white man's clothes. Seeing that, they forced all the young men to go to school and get some 'save', so they would go out and get jobs.

The jobs in prospect were white men's jobs, in town.[27] Villagers did not want those who left school to return to the village to work; they had no need of school to do that. White men's jobs were the prize the world over. The father, in Trinidad who had dreamed of his schoolboy son becoming a lawyer, or doctor, had no use for a good-for-nothing out picking cocoa. It was no good the son saying there were no other jobs to be had. He had been to school, and it was not necessary to have been to school to pick cocoa. Michael Anthony's 'Pa' will not listen to a good-for-nothing: 'What is cocoa-picking? Nobody does have to have brains for that. Why you don't look for something where it have to have brains!'[38] The Port Moresby fisherman would have been no less angry and frustrated than his Port of Spain counterpart in a similar situation. Faith in the wage and prestige-earning returns from schooling was immense; and it came from watching whites who had 'made it' – who had been to school, and who, in consequence, did not have to 'slave their guts out' in order to earn good money. These are the words of the novelist Witi Ihimaera, in the mouth of another father, a New Zealand Maori, to his brother: '. . . You got a big family. Get them educated. Boy, that's the story. My kids are going to get some brains. I want them to have better than I had. Easier than slaving your guts out. Me and Hine, we been working all our lives and we end up with nothing. You got to go where the money is. That's the Pakeha (white man's) way.'[29]

It was of no use for the headmaster of a so-called community school to appeal to the community for support, if education 'did not lead directly to wage-employment for successful students'.[30] Fees had been paid, and compensation was in order. The failure of the investment led to frustration, and even, as Katu writes, to 'hatred and distrust' of the 'dropouts', of education in general, and of primary (or community) schools, in particular.[31]

Fortunately, for the investors, and their investment, there were jobs to be had in the 1960s, the early days of large-scale government schooling. In those years mission and government schools were combined in one system, secondary schools mushroomed in all districts, manpower planning was high on the agenda, and development was the password in the corridors of the public service. A process of 'localisation' was set in motion, at a pace thought to preserve 'reasonable standards of efficiency'.[32] Schools were built to produce a qualified workforce; the situations vacant whetted demand for more schooling; and more and more schools were built to satisfy this demand. There were seven provincial high schools in 1960 (that is, secondary schools, nationally, for 13–16 year olds); by 1975, there were seventy-eight.[33] These schools had to be staffed. They were staffed either by teachers imported from Australia, New Zealand and the Phillipines, or by teachers drafted from the primary schools. Either way, there was a call for graduates of the school system to train as teachers, with all speed. Happily, such graduates were willing enough to continue their studies to this end. All it needed was a Grade 8 leaving-certificate, in those days, to qualify for one of the (mission-run) primary teachers' colleges. Research into the occupational choices of Grade 10 leavers from high schools in the Southern Highlands revealed that thirty per cent wished to enter teaching, and this was the preference of a still bigger proportion of the girls.[34] A conscious policy of localisation throughout the public service meant that more and more jobs, at technician, clerical, and executive levels were open to black school-leavers qualified to occupy them.[35] The days of school-leaver unemployment were in the future. The towns were expanding, there were jobs for labourers on building sites, for shop assistants in the stores, Carpenters and Steamships, for forecourt attendants at petrol stations, and for waiters in the sea-front hotels. Schooling did deliver the goods in those days, because the link between a school-leaving certificate and the most sought-after jobs, was clear-cut, and understood. 'Bush kanakas' could help build roads, and clear building sites; a Grade six certificate was good for a number of clean-handed jobs; and a Grade eight certificate was a pass to white-collar, white skin employment of the most coveted kind. The demand for certificates at Grades 10 and 12 came later. It is no wonder, with eighty-five per cent of Grade 6 school-leavers wanting to continue schooling beyond the primary level,[36] that headmasters had to turn hopefuls away in large numbers: eighteen year-olds wanting to enter Grade 2; and Grade 6 leavers wanting to repeat the year because they had failed to secure places at the secondary level.[37]

Certificates aside, what employers looked for, naturally enough, were basic bookkeeping skills, and a working knowledge of spoken and written English. Arithmetic was taught from the beginning, of course, often to the confusion of both teachers and pupils. Mathematical activity in the villages was at a discount;[38] numbers did not come easily to children whose parents still regarded reading and arithmetic as 'white man's magic'.[39] But too many white men knew that for their black employees to know some mathematics was good for business, for mathematics to be in any danger in the schools. Science, too, was perceived as giving access to control of magical forces, rather than as the entirely new way of apprehending natural phenomena that it was.[40] In spite of such misconceptions, or perhaps because of them, there was an undoubted hunger among pupils and their families, for courses in economics and commerce. Writing in 1976, Smyth looked back to 1967, when economics was first introduced as an elective subject in secondary schools, and reported a nine-fold increase in the choice of this subject (soon eclipsing history and geography), compared to a three-fold increase in overall secondary school enrolment.[41] Chatterton recalls a bookkeeping course that he gave in Port Moresby, that proved so popular, he had to repeat it, in one-week intensive bursts for allcomers. He put this down to 'the preoccupation of the younger folk with money'.[45]

The same preoccupation lay somewhere behind the demand for an English language-based, 'academic' education. Oram referred to the migration of villagers from Hula, to Port Moresby town, in the 1950s, on account of the government schools there. English was believed to be better taught at these schools than in the mission schools back in the village.[43] Agard reported the failure of the 'Skulanka' and 'Community Secondary Education' programmes, both designed to give the familiar 'rural bias' to an alternative form of secondary schooling.[44] Public opinion in PNG held the view no less dearly than in West Africa, that: 'even a starving professional was nearer to the kingdom of heaven than the most successful artisan . . .'[45]

The programmes failed because parents demanded that the academic content of the curricula be upgraded, at the expense of village-based content. If these schools were to be second chance secondary schools, parents were determined that the chance would be exploited for all it was worth. One of the last Australian administrators of education in PNG, McNamara, was forced to admit that efforts to 'turn the eyes of the children, the parents, and the teachers away from high school selection', had miscarried – as they had in numberless other countries.[46] What Oram described as happening in Port Moresby, Koroma noted of Goroka, in the Eastern Highlands. There, students from among the Bundi people were migrating from the village, into town, in order to acquire proficiency in English[47] – and it happened elsewhere. Parents sent their children to live with relatives in towns, rather than have them attend mission schools in the villages, and the reason was that government teachers taught in English, whilst mission teachers taught in Pidgin. Education itself had come close to being discredited in the late 1930s and '40s, because mission schooling was not delivering the goods. It was being seen, as Mclaren says, either as 'a hoax, or worse, a sop'.[48] Inasmuch as the missionaries taught in Pidgin, the people suspected that they were concealing the cargo secrets, and that they were doing this quite deliberately. And this in spite of the fact that many of the missionaries would have been quite capable of teaching in the vernacular,[49] and that Chatterton for one obstinately did.[50] Pidgin was a half-way house on a road that wound back to the village. An old man complained to the researcher, Wootten: 'They did not show us the straight road that would lead us on to your knowledge, your ideas, your language . . .'[51]

Faith was restored in education only when the white man's language opened up a straight road to jobs. At this early stage, there was little of the linguistic nationalism in PNG that had begun to take root in certain of the more 'developed' ex-colonies. Generations old and young in PNG left a concern for the survival of vernacular languages to foreign scholars. It was too soon to weigh an unfelt loss in the balance with all that might be gained from learning English.

Fluency in English was a prerequisite for salaried employment, as teachers, pupils, and their parents well knew. The government schools of the 1960s were besieged by seekers after 'real' education of the sort tht would confer 'paua' – not to say glory; for English was as well-cut a key to prestige as four-wheel drive. The Papuans could speak English, whilst the Chimbus could not. The result (as Kondom, a Chimbu chief put it), was that 'the Papuans get all the good jobs, and use the Chimbus to dig dams and collect rubbish'.[52] The Kuanua-speaking Tolais were at the same disadvantage, in Port Moresby; the Papuans were up at the front of the job queues; and this is what counted, whatever Chatterton, and Hueter,[53] and others like them (English-speakers all) might say. Certainly English was a 'cargo' language, as the latter suggested, and who can wonder? Opeba interviewed a fifty year-old prophetess who claimed to have witnessed heaven and the after-life. She told him: 'When one dies and departs, he joins the company of other people from the villages . . . They leave their original earthy body and are all white by the time they press through to this stage. They immediately adopt the *Inglis* language; those who were not educated were put immediately into schools . . .'[54]

Two Grade 10 students, both destined for higher education, had this to say:

> Since I am in grade 10 and am big enough to think for myself, the feeling I have towards education is that it was for my parents' sake that they sent me to school, so that I can read and write and contact white people for something they wanted, or to translate the white man's language to my parents. (Sigizanto Soyava)

> My people believe that education is the gateway to our dead ancestors. They believe that if they sent their kids to school, the kids may learn the

basic ideas and the secrets of the white men. Once these lads are able to read, write and understand the white man's language, they will be able to communicate with their dead ancestors and have some business trade among them, in order to become rich. (B'Zogarefa Aveke)

Chatterton knew well enough that English had become a cargo cult;[55] this is one reason why he refused to promote it. Alkan Tololo, Minister of Education knew it too ('There is a semi-magical belief that speaking and writing English like Europeans means the possession of many goods and much power'[56]) but his recipe was more education, not less. Hoiri, the eponymous hero of Vincent Eri's novel *The Crocodile*, began to question why he was at school. He: 'felt vaguely that he wanted to learn the white man's language. Not because he wanted to get a well-paid job – for there weren't any such jobs for Papuans and New Guineans to fill – but because the ability to converse with the white people would earn him a respected position in the eyes of the community.'[57]

Of course, familiarity bred contempt. Just as a growing knowledge of the white man reduced him to less than a god, so more education went some way towards demythologising the English language. A sort of grade inflation was at work, devaluing each successive stage of education, as increasing numbers graduated. This is the common currency of experience in 'emergent' countries: that primary education in the vernacular cedes prestige to primary education in English; and this, in its turn, is upstaged by lower secondary education; and this, by upper secondary education. The employment market bore the primary responsibility for this grade inflation in many African countries; and, to be sure, employers demanded more and more sophisticated qualifications in Papua New Guinea, and this demand from above quickened the demand from below, on the part of pupils and their parents. But the spiral of cargoist expectations added to the rate of inflation in the Papua New Guinea context. The English language was only one of a series of steps on the spiral. Baptism, church services, neat gardens, flowers on tables, drilling in lines and going to school had been steps at the bottom, and every year of schooling had been one step more. But there was still quite a long way to the top of the tower. The provoking thing was that every time a step was taken, more came into view. The more one knew, the more there seemed to be to know.

One step beyond high school was the university. If English was a cargo cult, the University of Papua New Guinea came to be the temple of the cult: it lay low on virgin land well beyond the outliers of Port Moresby; it was more brick and timber than glass and tile; more academic village than company headquarters, but a symbol, and a source of pride nevertheless. UPNG opened its doors to Grade 10 leavers in 1966. Just as the high hopes that had been vested in the first children from the village to attend mission school had then been fastened on the first Grade 6 leavers to leave home for boarding school, perhaps many miles away, so now they were transferred to the young man (or less often the young woman) who would represent the village – or the district, or the secondary school – at what must surely be the top of the tower. The Nigerian novelist Nkem Nwankwo speaks of the first undergraduates at Lagos University: 'The first students were few and enjoyed all the privileges of rarity. The country made much of them, denied them nothing.'[58] Something similar might be said of the first plants bedded out in the hothouse that was the University of Papua New Guinea.

Even as the Administrator, Mr D. O. Hay, was opening new buildings on the campus, in 1969, he warned that the university should not be regarded as a 'temple of some universal cargo cult'.[59] But the warning was too late; what is more, it was being issued to the wrong audience. The people who Mr Hay feared would misapprehend the purposes of the university, were beyond his urbane words, in a thousand and one villages. In village primary schools, children sang out numbers and letters for all to hear. The school was an integral part of the village, built by the village, as like as not, and almost comprehensible. High school was more of a mystery, more obviously alien, of fibro-boarding – a village in itself, with its dormitories, and its offices, and staff houses, and cars. But the high school was no more than a public taxi fare away. It could be got at, and gaped at, and the learning that went on there could be guessed at. But the University, to which students had to fly, was beyond any villager's knowing. Ebia Olewale, Tololo's predecessor at the Education ministry, was well aware how big a mystery the University was to the parents of its students. He wrote in 1972: 'The University is causing tension because the village people do not know what their children are doing.'[60]

The tension was not lessened when those 'children' went home, with money in their pockets, and gifts for their families. Students were paid pocket money for the duration of their course, money that was wealth to most, but which was as nothing to what they could earn as graduates. The young had never had so much money before, nor yet the material assets that money could buy. Mature men had wielded the power and the influence before;[61] they were the ones who had dominated the men's house and the councils of war; they were the ones who had owned all the objects of any value.[62] Now it was money that was most highly prized (because negotiable), and this was in the hands, and the gift, of young men. They returned to the village from the university, or a job in the capital, with suitcases full of shirts, and bolts of cloth, and torches, and cigarettes, and sun-glasses, and sandals and soft biscuits – city gifts that the old men could not match. It would have been problem enough that young people who had been to school had an advantage over their age-mates who had not; but in the Papua New Guinea context, it was a still greater problem that the young won a never to be gainsaid advantage over the old. As status had been associated with giving, and reciprocating, so the old men dropped out of the competition. Young men were not merely the new rich; they were the only rich; the old had been superseded.

The tension bred a certain bitterness. Chatterton spoke of the 'apple of affluence' that the young were biting into;[63] but it was not all sweetness to the core. Vulliamy, writing of the new style community secondary schools, has referred to the diffidence among 'numerous students . . . afraid to start a project in their villages for fear of jealousy and magic'.[64] How much more conscious must university students, and graduates, have been of the danger of disturbing a hornets' nest of sorcery, as a result of their own more sophisticated experiments in fiscal evangelism. White men, too, might take the shine off the apple, jealous of their threatened monopoly; Eri could put this warning into the mouth of one of his fictional, educated natives: 'it's their schools and their language, and it can hardly be expected of them to be over-generous. Even if they were, it is dangerous to absorb it all. Many of you have heard of the tragic ends of our friends who became as clever as the white men before their time.'[65] There was 'poison' in the apple if you bit too deep.

References

[1]Lawrence (1964), pp. 88, 89.
[2]Oliver (1973), pp. 151, 152.
[3]Smith, Richard A., 'Discontinuities in education at Wankung' in Brammall & May (1975), p. 346 ff.
[4]Strathern (1972), p. 229.
[5]University of Papua New Guinea (1976), p. 29.
[6]Waiba, Joseph, 'Lumi WSP' in Weeks (1978), p. 180.
[7]Palmer (1978), p. 37.
[8]Monson, Joseph, 'Education and rural development in the Southern Highlands' in Powell & Wilson (1974).
[9]Stanton, Ron, 'Secondary schools community extension project' in Department of Education (1979).
[10]Conroy (1972).
[11]Okara, Gabriel, *The Voice*, London, Heinemann Educational Books (1970), p. 58.
[12]quoted by Michael Dangu, of the Chimbu Province, in Weeks (1977), p. 19.
[13]Giraure, Nelson, 'The need for a cultural programme' in Brammall & May (1975).
[14]Steinbauer (1974), p. 40.
[15]Epstein (1969), p. 318.
[16]Morauta (1974), p. 125.
[17]Smith (1974), p. 133.
[18]Department of Education (1979), p. 12.
[19]Nelson (1974), p. 177.
[20]Weeks (1977), p. 105.
[21]Kaunda, Kenneth, *Zambia shall be Free*, London, Heinemann Educational Books (1962), p. 9.
[22]Finney (1973), pp. 80, 81.
[23]Weeks (1978), p. 72.
[24]McGregor (1976), p. 191.
[25]Clarke (1975), p. 23.
[26]Oliver (1973), p. 195.
[27]Bais, Tony, 'Agarabi vocational centre, Kainantu sub-district' in Powell & Wilson (1974), p. 12.
[28]Anthony, Michael, *Green Days By The River*, London, Heinemann Educational Books (1973).
[29]Ihimaera, Witi, *Pounamu Pounamu*, Auckland, William Heinemann Ltd (1972), p. 66.
[30]Lancy (1979), p. 97.
[31]Katu, Peter, 'Siassi Island, Morobe' in Weeks (1978), p. 144.
[32]Langmore, John, 'Public service pay and localization policy' in Clunies-Ross & Langmore (1973), p. 207.
[33]Vulliamy (1980), p. 7.
[34]University of Papua New Guinea (1976), pp. 16, 17.

[35] Oram (1976), p. 146.

[36] Conroy, J. D., 'The impact of education: an African model applied to PNG' in Thomas (1976), p. 81.

[37] Nelson (1974), p. 177.

[38] Roberts (1977), p. 9.

[39] White (1965), p. 165.

[40] Young (1977), p. 21.

[41] Smyth (1976), p. 3.

[42] Chatterton (1974), p. 69.

[43] Oram, N. D., 'The Hula in Port Moresby' in May (1977), p. 132.

[44] Agard (1978), p. 41.

[45] Conton, William, *The African*, London, Heinemann Educational Books (1964), p. 87.

[46] McNamara, V., 'High school selection, and the breakdown of village society' in Thomas (1976), p. 68.

[47] Koroma, Joseph, 'A study of the Bundi people in urban Goroka' in May (1977), p. 204.

[48] McClaren, Peter, 'Schools and knowledge in Astrolabe Bay' in Brammall & May (1975), p. 359.

[49] Lawrence (1964), p. 56.

[50] Chatterton (1974), p. 50.

[51] Rowley (1965), p. 166.

[52] Smith (1975), p. 50.

[53] Hueter, Irene, 'Why English – Why not Pidgin?' in Weeks (1976), p. 59.

[54] Opeba, Willington Jojoya, 'The "Peroveta" of Buna' in Trompf (1977), p. 231.

[55] Chatterton (1974), p. 51.

[56] Tololo, Alkan, 'A consideration of some likely future trends in education in PNG' in Brammall & May (1975), p. 11.

[57] Eri (1973), p. 4.

[58] Nwankwo, Nkem, *My Mercedes is Bigger than Yours*, London, André Deutsch (1975), p. 21.

[59] Griffin, James, 'The instant university' in Thomas (1976), p. 99.

[60] Olewale, Ebia, 'The impact of the University on village communities' in Thomas (1976), p. 124.

[61] Burridge (1969), p. 114.

[62] Hogbin (1951), p. 184.

[63] Chatterton (1974), p. 119.

[64] Vulliamy (1980), p. 42.

[65] Eri (1973), p. 101.

6

The awakening

In 1966, there were no more than 353 school-leavers, countrywide, with a School or Senior Certificate (that is, a present-day Grade 10 – or in U.K. terms, an O-level – Certificate), or something higher.[1] These were all that there were of what Beltz called 'better-educated indigenes', to occupy positions of authority in commerce and the public service.[2] At a time when the country was being prepared for self-government, there was little or no educated élite. It was expected that the number of certificate holders would rise to 12,000 by 1973; yet already, in this latter year, Sheehan could wonder whether the school system was not dividing the one nation-to-be into two nations of the schooled and the unschooled. 'If the competitive consumer society requires an educated élite, a privileged group with access to the most sophisticated consumer goods, the most extended and expensive education . . . then that is being achieved.'

'Also being achieved,' Sheehan wrote, 'is a high rate of dropping out, repetition of grades, and a total absence of any schooling opportunity for large numbers of people . . .'[3] Particularly worrying was the fact that the bright new universities in Port Moresby and Lae were recruiting handsomely, but lower level institutions, and the apprenticeship system, were failing to produce technicians, clerks, and others with qualifications of an intermediate sort. Speed was vital, but dangerous. No one doubted that education was in order – self-government could not now be granted to a 'thousand tribes' – yet formal schooling was not producing a manpower fit to govern or be governed. By the end of the ten years of expansion 1961–71, half the children of school age (approximately 241,000 of them) were in mission and administration schools, twice as many as had been at school at the beginning of the decade. Yet only just over ten per cent of these children were receiving post-primary education, and of the rest, 'the majority could be expected to leave before they had achieved effective literacy in either English or Pidgin'.[4] Those who had advocated a great leap forward had not seen the mud.

One especially nasty patch was that which lay between urban and rural districts. There appeared to be good grounds for favouring the towns where investment in schools was concerned: urban children needed to be literate and numerate (to a degree) to earn a living wage; rural children, heirs to the subsistence economy of the village, had no urgent need of more than domestic skills. Furthermore, formal schooling in the village would add to the drift to the towns already under way. These arguments for inequity were advanced by no less a body than the Urban Synod of the United Church.[5] It was also pointed out that it was a good deal more expensive to build schools in the rural areas, than in the towns.[6] Thousands of one-teacher schools would be needed if the demands of every bush village were to be met. The drain on resources was unthinkable. In the Highlands and New Guinea coastal regions barely twenty-five per cent of school-age children were in full time education; yet the rate of population growth in the Highlands and Sepik districts was higher than in the Islands, and on the Papuan coast, where nearly all the age group was in school. Nowhere were arguments from equity so much in conflict with those from efficiency as in pre-independence Papua New Guinea. But because the country was moving towards independence, and because elected representatives of the Central, Sepik, Southern Highlands, Gulf, and all other districts were meeting together for the first time in the House of Assembly, and comparing notes, there was no alternative but to accede to some, at least, of the demands of those members who clamoured for fair shares. Thus, it was official policy, in the early 'seventies, to provide primary school places in each district for up to fifty per cent of the relevant age group, within the shortest possible time. Meanwhile, there would be no reduction in the proportion of children at school in those districts already ahead of this target.[7] This was the policy that seemed to make most planning sense. Planners said it was all the country could afford, but politicians thought otherwise. Those representing Highlands constituencies could see for themselves how much catching up there was to do. They had not been elected to the House of Assembly to settle for fifty per cent. The consequence of fifty per cent development was fifty per cent under-development, fifty per cent backwardness, fifty per cent 'paua', fifty per cent of the cargo.

Years of contact with Europeans gave Papuans the edge over their upcountry compatriots. Port Moresby had been visibly 'developed' earlier than elsewhere: Australia was a hundred miles over the water; there were jobs there, English was spoken, and cargo was unloaded at the wharf with bills of lading from Sydney. Sophisticated Tolais from New Britain sought and found mainly government posts in the capital, but, as Rowley points out, they met their match and something more among the Papuans. Papuan leaders had the advantage of a longer experience of reading and speaking English, and this gave them 'a window on the world denied the Tolai, whose leaders with few exceptions (knew) Pidgin but not English'.[8] The inequality between coastals and highlanders, however, was still more gross, and consciousness of it could give rise to nasty incidents. One such occurred on Saturday 21 July 1973, when teams from New Guinea and Papua met to play an inter-territory rugby league match at the Hubert Murray Stadium in Port Moresby. The defeat of the New Guineans led to rioting throughout the city which was only finally quelled by policy on the Sunday. Clarke says of this incident that: 'the main causes seemed to be the frustration of unemployed or lowly paid, illiterate Highlanders compared with the relative affluence of many of the educated Papuans.'[9]

Much faith had been placed in the new local government councils, instituted in the late 1950s; expectation ran high that the 'Konsel' would mitigate such inequality – at least, it did in New Guinea. Local government councils came to the Chimbu in 1959. Leading councillors evangelised in a thoroughgoing fashion, preaching co-operation, the learning of new skills, coffee-growing, and the support of government schools.[10] In Madang, the councils enjoyed the active backing of the church. Being a good Christian was associated with being a good citizen, paying taxes, and supporting the council. Council meetings opened in prayer, and certain classes of church workers were granted automatic tax reductions.[11] But the councils were not welcomed everywhere with such enthusiasm: the very word 'council' could evoke memories of the council which put Jesus Christ to death. Where the people were opposed to the central government, they expressed no less opposition to government at the local level – not because they were anti-church, but because they believed the government was anti-church. Matane speaks of popular suspicion of the council's motives. It was supposed that a tax on their incomes would be followed by expropriation of their land, and prohibition of their forms of worship.[12] The Hahalis people on Buka Island wanted a school, and an aid post. They petitioned the government for a teacher and a 'doctor boy', promising to supply all other necessities themselves. When this request was ignored, one Keari had no difficulty persuading the people that 'since the government did nothing for them, they owed nothing to the government . . .'[13] Accordingly, Keari and a relative, John Teosin, founded the Hahalis Welfare Society on the self-help principle. This society became something of a cause célèbre, so it bears pointing out that there was more than one view of its means and ends. We have met John Teosin before, as a student expected to learn cargo secrets at school in Rabaul (see above, p. 87). The connection between politics and cargo-cultism has been well made, not least by Ted Diro, native Major of the Pacific Islands Regiment, in Port Moresby. 'Quite often,' he writes, 'it is the man who can deliver the goods who is elected and stays elected.'[14] Naturally enough, the government supposed that the Hahalis Welfare Society was just another cargo cult, and represented it as such. Former Police Inspector John Banono Hihina could confidently report as follows: 'In 1962 we had trouble at Hahalis on Buka Island, where John Teosin, Francis Hagai, and the old Sawa started a cargo cult. About 2,000 members joined it, and the situation was rather awkward.' It was so 'awkward' indeed ('people did not attend church any more, and began to hate the government and refused to pay taxes') that there was a fight, '700 natives' had to be arrested, and a further 200 had to be charged with a failure to pay taxes.[15] According to Kiki, however, the Society's leaders did not believe in the cargo. Their object was to organize communal farming, and to do this they needed access to the land held by village elders whose belief in ritual was stronger than their belief, and investment, in hard work. Teosin among others knew that the elders would release their land for the common good only if they could be persuaded that in so doing, they would expedite the coming of the cargo. Thus, meetings of the Society were held in the cemetery, in an atmosphere heavy with wonder, and expectancy. According to Kiki, 'none of the young people involved in the movement believed in anything but hard work, but they were forced to please their elders'.[16] It matters little how many members of the Society ('rebels' is Hihina's word for them) believed or did not believe in the coming of the cargo; what is significant (in Oliver's non-partisan view) is that this movement was not only anti-government, it was also anti-church. In this context, the church was the Catholic Marist Church, and the chief grievance of the Buka people where the Catholics were concerned was that converts had been given catechisms only, in place of the Bible in all its Holy completeness. The Hahalis Welfare Society conducted services of its own, 'which included Bible reading, hymn singing and prayers to God via the members' own ancestral spirits'.[17] Buka had witnessed the building and opening up of two new roads to the cargo – government and church – and they had shown themselves willing to travel these roads. But both had been blocked. So the people had chosen a government, and had founded a church, of their own. Their 'rebellion' did not signal despair, or dimming of the 'cargo' vision – on the contrary; it was a reaffirmation of their faith in European means to European ends.

There was an intimate relationship between economic development and cultism. Gorokans, in the Eastern Highlands, enjoyed the profits of a buoyant market for their coffee, and in consequence, cult activity of a ritualistic kind was at a low level. This is not to say that coffee-growing was not itself seen as a 'road belong cargo'; after all, copper-mining was seen as such in Bougainville. There had been cult activity on the island before copper was discovered in economic quantities, and before the Company moved in. Cultists near Teop had been apprehended in 1959, in a plot to murder the local missionary; they blamed his prayers for delaying the arrival of cargo. And in similar circumstances, the mission station at Keriaka was looted, and the priest was obliged to flee for his life, in 1960.[18]

Several business ventures were floated in the mid-sixties, some of them on a genuinely commercial basis, and others on a cushion of high hopes. Many were a mixture of rational economics, and ritualism – all were motivated by what Oliver calls a 'widespread and seemingly undauntable' enthusiasm for making money.[19] The Copper Company was careful to damp down cargoist expectations of the mine: it merely offered jobs, a big hole, restitution in due course, and a percentage of the profits to the government in Port Moresby. It could not foresee that young men would forsake the land, young women would turn to prostitution, old customs would be undermined, and established values overthrown. Bougainville natives witnessed the destruction of field and forest by gluttonous machines, monstrous diggers gouging ancestral land, buildings erected in days, white mineworkers the worse for liquor, 'redskins' from the mainland with fat wallets, and a steady flow of ships and planes, loading and unloading the stuff of dreams. Hastings was in no doubt (in 1969) that the Bougainville Copper Company was a 'giant cargo cult, for nothing seems beyond its competence – roads, schools, hospital, trade stores, cinema, supermarket, housing, markets . . .'[20] Bougainville in the 'sixties was like Manus in the 'forties all over again.

There were those with reservations about the pace of development, and the costs that it would impose. The Tolai people of Matupit Island, New Britain, for example, were eager for education. In particular, they wanted their children to learn English like the Papuans, to be able to compete for jobs, and raise the standing of the island in the eyes of the Europeans. But they were unwilling to surrender scarce land for the building of a teacher's house.[21] Land was for the Tolais what it was to the Kikuyu of Kenya. The Tolai had not suffered like the Kikuyu, and they could see for themselves that the dwindling Gazelle was as much under threat from their own population growth, as from European land hunger. They sought education because without it, they would be ill-equipped for the town that was engulfing them.

Parents in the Highlands were anxious not to sacrifice control over their daughters' choice of marriage partners, and thus the size of the bride-price, on the altar of equal opportunity. If progress meant the loss of this substantial receipt of cash and kind, it threatened to be too expensive.[22] But the more perceptive recognised the benefits of development; their worry was that these benefits were not being fairly distributed. There were disparities between those being secured for coastal peoples and those for highlanders; between those for the educated and those for the uneducated; and between those for townspeople, and those for villagers. But these disparities were as nothing compared to the huge imbalance between the poverty of urban natives, and the flaunted wealth of the Europeans. Such urban natives were leaving school in growing numbers with eyes opened to see the imbalance, minds educated to understand it, and expectations sharpened to resent it. They stalked the towns looking for jobs, armed with Grade 6 and Grade 8 leaving certificates. They saw the shop windows of Port Moresby, Rabaul, Lae and Wewak filled with all that the young might covet – with all that (even if they found work) their small savings would never buy. The smart clothes, the toiletries, the household gadgets, the imported foods and drink – these were not for them. They could no more think of stocking a fridge than they could of living on the hill above Port Moresby's Ela Beach. Todd understood this envy, and the resentment to which it gave rise, and recognised that this was what 'provided the embryo, soon to grow into a giant, of the demand for self-government'.[23]

The first general election to be held in Papua New Guinea was in 1964. The Australian administration spent a year preparing people for the event, explaining what it was for, and what it would involve. Constituencies were defined, short lists of candidates were drafted, and the House of Assembly, and the duties of a member of the house were all painstakingly described. Perhaps it was this very thorough preparation, and the seriousness with which the administration invested the election, that gave voters-to-be the impression that it would change the course of their lives, like Christianity, and education. It cannot have been a cause for surprise, but it might well have been a cause for chagrin, that natives looked to the election as the means by which they would at last learn the secret of the cargo. They still had hopes that attendance at church and school would give them the 'save' (the knowledge) that they sought, but this knowledge was still at the whim of the white man – the white priest, and the white schoolteacher (or black ones, answerable to white bishops and white ministers). Now, for the first time, they were being promised power in their own hands. They would have access, through their own men, to the place where decisions were made.

Lawrence was in no doubt that cargoism lay at the back of popular beliefs about the election in the East Sepik and Madang Districts.[24] Woolford reports widespread evidence of a super-stitious apprehension of the event: there were those tribesmen who thought it proper to abstain from sexual intercourse before voting, as they might before fighting, that their manhood might not be impaired; there were those who feared to stand for election, lest they be thought big-headed, and suffer sorcery; and there were those groups in the Highlands who held purification rites with pigs' blood before registering their vote.[25] Yali's followers in Madang had particularly colourful ideas of what the House of Assembly was all about. They thought of it as a 'haus tambaran' (or cult house) to end all such houses. It had a door which only Yali, the 'King of New Guinea' could open, since there were whirling swords on it which would rest only at Yali's approach. This, it was presumed, was the meaning of the term 'Rai Coast Open Electorate'. When he opened this door, riches would pour out for all New Guinea.[26]

The administration, quite unwittingly, had itself supplied some of the ingredients for these ideas. Before the war, the Catholic Mission had bought artefacts from the local people, and so had incurred Yali's wrath for stealing the local gods. Now, at the same time as officials toured the country instructing people about the new parliament, they asked them to send masks and other carvings to the Anthropological Museum on the lower ground floor of the House of Assembly. It was no great matter for Yali to convince his followers that their cult deities were being stolen from them once again, and being installed in the white man's cult house in Port Moresby. That Yali was not elected, was evidence to those who had voted for him, that the Europeans were not going to keep their promises after all. They had given converts to Christianity an incomplete Bible, and they had taught Pidgin English (in the mission schools) in place of the real thing. Now, it seemed, the essential part of political power was to be withheld also; young and timid members, with a little book learning, but no schooling in European guile (such as Yali had) were to sit in the House and be overpowered. This suspicion was confirmed, when what came to be regarded as the instrument of European power, the mace (the 'tambaran' itself), was monopolised by the European speaker of the House, H. R. Niall.[27] What more evidence was needed of the whiteman's trickery than this?

But it took time for disillusionment such as this to set in. Electors in 1964 had high hopes of their members. Writers on the subject agree that the vast majority of those who voted did so in the belief that those for whom they cast their vote would secure material benefits for their constituents.[28] Stoi Umul campaigned openly on a cargoist platform, in Madang. His successful chain of trade stores was evidence enough that he was on the right road.[29] The constituents of Lavongai, New Ireland, left even less room to doubt their motives: they interpreted the invitation to choose any candidate they pleased, quite literally. The Germans, the Japanese, the Australians, all had come to Lavongai, but none of these had pleased the islanders. They had done nothing to bring development to the island. So, in the belief that the Americans would please them better, the good people of Lavongai chose the then president of the United States as their candidate – Lyndon B. Johnson.

In one respect, the electors were not disappointed in their members. If a native member stood up to speak in the House of Assembly, it was almost certainly to ask for roads and schools – primary schools at first, and later on, high schools.[30] Nelson says of the speakers in this first parliament (especially if they were from the Highlands), that 'they made a statement of gratitude to Australia, pleaded for opportunities to enter the cash economy, and asked for roads, bridges and schools'.[31] Members regarded their peers as rivals in a competition for development projects. He who spoke longest and loudest would be heard, heeded, and re-elected. And this is how it was until late into the night of November 1967, when the house adjourned (in Nelson's words) 'amid last-minute pleas for roads and schools . . .'.[32] That the appeal to cargoist expectation was less overt, and less successful, in the 1968 elections than in 1964, is due in part to the fact that roads and airstrips *were* built, and schools and medical aid posts *were* established where they were most needed. Younger voters had been disabused of some of the more colourful visions of their elders, by a little down-to-earth teaching in school, and optimism about their own future as wage earners. A New Guinea coast road gave villagers access to markets for the sale of the surplus of their food gardens, and their cash crops; and for the purchase of material goods in the urban trade stores. That a little of the cargo was now within reach blunted the appeal of Yali, and that of those of his kind who preached white perfidy and black magic. Harding and Lawrence make the point, however, that cargoism was 'convincingly defeated' in the second Rai Coast Open election, not because cargoism was on the wane, but because no candidate in the constituency under investigation (Kabwum) 'sought to mobilise cargoist support as Stoi had done in the first election'.[33] This does not mean that the support was not there; cargoist assumptions were still very much alive – indeed, in 1971, cult activity could impinge on central government politics to the extent of upsetting the electoral calculations of the member who was campaigning most vigorously for self-government, and who would lead the Pangu Pati to victory, and office, at independence – Michael Somare. Mathias Yaliwan had foretold the coming of cargo, and in so doing had captured the imagination of thousands of natives in the East Sepik. Somare could write off Yaliwan as a man 'disturbed by dreams and visions', and his movement as 'absurd',[34] but he knew well enough that a vital seat was under threat. His colleagues advised him that it would be 'politically unwise' to oppose Yaliwan, for fear of alienating the voters in his own, neighbouring electorate. But Somare's view was that he 'had no choice but to take the risk involved'. He opposed him, and Yaliwan was returned as the M.H.A. for Yangoru. Furthermore, the sitting member for the Wewak Open electorate, Mr Beibi Yambanda, made no secret of his enrolment in Yaliwan's cult. He paid fourteen dollars to join – ten dollars for himself, and two dollars for each of his two wives.[35]

Cult activity seized even coffee-rich Goroka, in 1973. Gough Whitlam, leader of the Australian Labour Party, was a prime minister more sympathetic towards territorial self-determination than his Liberal Party predecessor had been. February 1973 found him on tour in the New Guinea Highlands, impressing all who saw him by his commanding presence. Todd describes him as being six feet six inches tall, and weighing 'the best part of 250 pounds'. Sheer size was a qualification for leadership in the Eastern Highlands, and for the status of 'big man'. Whitlam was quite clearly a big man, and equally clearly, he was a man in a hurry. The

Liberal government had promised that self-government would be granted when a majority of the people voted for it. Whitlam had only been in office two months, and already he was in New Guinea promising self-government 'as quickly as possible'.[36] Another man who wasted no time between thought and deed, was a local village chief. He organized what he called the Gopp Guard (a corruption of Gough), of one hundred fully-feathered warriors, armed to the dogs' teeth with bows and arrows. This formidable bodyguard would fly to Canberra, to escort Mr Whitlam on all his travels, in exchange for one hundred planeloads of cargo for the families of the guards. The offer was not taken up, but it might well have suggested to Mr Whitlam that he pause for thought.

Everyone, Highlanders, islanders, and coastals wanted economic development, whether this was understood in millenarian, or western capitalist terms. But not everyone wanted independence. A number of politicians and their constituents in the Highlands, in particular, were worried that early independence would jeopardize their chances of catching up with their compatriots on the coast. The white man, the churches, schools, roads, trade stores, and job opportunities had all come late to the Highlands. Now that they had come, the Australians who had provided them were threatening to pull out, taking their language and their book-learning, their businesses and their know-how with them. Highlanders feared that if the Australians left a vacuum in government, Papuans would fill it, and legislate in ways that suited them, and New Guineans would suffer permanent backwardness. This was a powerful case, and Somare's Pangu Pati had an uphill job to marshal arguments against it. Cargoists themselves were divided on the issue: one candidate in the 1968 elections had undertaken to raise 30,000 dollars as an inducement to the whites to stay (at least in New Britain) until such a time as the natives had learnt the cargo secret.[37] On the other hand, a cult official in Madang saw things in a different light: he told the anthropologist Morauta: 'I am still living in a grass hut. If self-government comes I shall have a good house, good chairs and a happy heart.'[38]

Much seemed to turn upon whether one was by nature optimistic or pessimistic. Certain Highlanders, unmoved by Pangu Pati rhetoric, remained pessimistic in the run up to independence, called themselves the United Party, and went into opposition after independence as pessimistic as ever. The Pangu Pati won the day because its leaders had judged correctly that, pessimists apart, people were ready to shrug off pupillage, and learn by doing. Once again, Somare rejected the advice given him by his fellow party leaders. They had counselled him to 'soft-peddle [sic] the issue of self-government', because it upset people; but he 'campaigned boldly' for it, saying to electors: 'You must know that I am a member of the Pangu Pati and Pangu wants early self-government. Let not others tell you that if self-government comes all white people will go. I know you have often been told that the Australians will suddenly leave and take all their cars and planes with them.'[39]

This boldness won Pangu (Papua New Guinea Union) the hearts and minds of a sufficient number of electors to enable it to enter into coalition with the small People's Progress Party under Julius Chan, forcing the pessimists into increasingly sterile opposition. Papua New Guinea was granted full independence in 1975, the year in which its patron, Gough Whitlam, was removed from office.

A Grade 10 student, Atatai Arebeba, asked his father what villagers had supposed independence would bring. His father (Arebeba) was a native of Norikori village in the Kainantu sub-district of what came to be called the Eastern Highlands Province. Atatai reported as follows: villagers believed that

> before getting independence these things would happen first: there'd be wars between Papua New Guinea and the ancestors. They believed that at the day of independence big planes would fly over P.N.G., one after the other. They believed that before all these things happened they would kill pigs, and get pig fat, and rub it on the roads everywhere so that the horses could walk on them with their cargoes. They believed after independence the villages would change into towns. When this happened they would be given everything free by the ancestors. Many people were excited by the things that were going to happen. They were so excited to have things free from their ancestors. They also believed that once a person had done something wrong, they would be killed by the ancestors after all these things had happened.
>
> This was in 1974–5. (On the day of independence) the people made feasts at the community centre and watched to see if the planes would come.
>
> These beliefs were first put about by the big men of the village.
>
> When people believed these things I told them things would not happen. I was in grade seven at Kainantu High School. We were told to

go back to our villages and celebrate Independence Day, but they didn't believe what I said. Almost the whole village believed these things – including my father.

There is no reason to suppose that Arebeba, or Norikori village, were unusual; and there are many indications that both represented subsistence farmers and small settlements, accounting for the vast majority of would-be Papua New Guineans.

The new government put forward an Eight Point Plan whose emphasis was on self-reliance, small-scale artisan production, decentralisation of power, the development of agriculture, social–economic equality, and the localisation of employment in the public and private sectors. There was nothing in the plan to which anyone could take justified exception; there was much in it that was thoughtful and forward-looking. There were those who thought it over-ambitious: John Kaputin, John Momis, Leo Hannett and others are said to have been 'enamoured of poor-but-proud, communalistic ideas', of a sort which distrusted the Australian capitalist inheritance. Such ideas did receive some recognition in the Point concerning self-reliance (this was a principle to which the government did commit itself quite consistently), but few people, peasants or politicians, entertained them in their full rigour. Even Kaputin and Momis accepted cabinet office when it was offered them, which suggests that they were prepared to compromise. But it may be that as ministers, their life-style was less at variance with the spirit of the Eight Points than that of their cabinet and parliamentary colleagues. Woolford speaks of the 'good homes, cars, and restaurants' that figure in the lives of national politicians and civil servants. He is careful not to charge the architects of the Eight Points with hypocrisy – indeed, he owns that 'many are probably unaware of the dichotomy in their own lives' – but he does have to conclude that 'the attractions of western affluence have proved too seductive for the egalitarian principles of the Eight Points to have much chance of success'.[40]

One western model that proved to be seductive was the primary school system. The outgoing administration left behind two sorts of primary schools: the 'A' (Australian curriculum) schools, and the 'T' (Territory curriculum) schools. The former taught wholly in English, and prepared its charges for the Queensland system of secondary education, and, to put it simply, the latter did not. White expatriates had established the 'A' schools for their own children, whose future, naturally enough, would be down south in Australia. But in so doing they had unwittingly put before Papua New Guineans what McKinnon called 'an alternative model of what a school should be'.[41] Thus, when correspondence in the *Post-Courier* newspaper (in 1978–9) was not lambasting government officials for undertaking costly trips abroad, and otherwise 'junketing' on the public account, it was reproaching Michael Somare for sending his children to Australian schools.

But the education debate really came to a head at the secondary level. It was essentially between those, like Alkan Tololo, Director of Education, who argued for 'a more appropriate type of education for Papua New Guinea' (than the Australian system), and those like the above-mentioned John Kaputin, Minister for Justice, who pointed out that: 'whether we aim to "reach the village or the moon", the language . . . is the same. We are not operating in a vacuum and, as a result, and whether we like it or not, we simply have to learn the language that this world speaks. Simply to master the arts of reading and writing is not enough . . .'[42]

To be fair, Tololo was not merely aiming to 'reach the village'; the aim of secondary education as he saw it was to 'provide an adequate preparation for post secondary training courses, direct employment needs, and for responsible participation in community life'.[43] The problem was – as it has been in all developing societies – that education was considered to be a good thing, and that more was considered to be better; that social demand for equal shares to education made satisfaction a political imperative; and yet that the country could not provide employment opportunities of a kind that would match the expectations of large numbers of school graduates (and their parents) with academic qualifications of the kind most in demand. Though the 1977 secondary enrolment represented only about twelve per cent of all children in the 12–16 age group, and though as many as forty per cent of the fourteen-year olds left school at the end of Grade 8, Tololo could still warn, even at this early stage, that:

> high school leavers are already exceeding training and employment requirements. An increasing proportion of grade eight and grade ten leavers will be underemployed or unemployed, and the Department shares a responsibility with parents, the community and other

agencies to ensure that these school leavers also become useful citizens.[44]

For its part, the Department revised the curriculum in Grades 7 and 8, to incorporate 'a substantial proportion of practical skills and agricultural activities in addition to regular academic skills'.[45] This revision was well meant, but it is noteworthy that the 'academic' skills were thought of as 'regular', and the practical skills as supplementary. It is to be compared with the provisions of the Community Secondary Education Project, inaugurated in 1973, for Grade 6 leavers too young to attend vocational centres. The CSE scheme aimed to 'provide a relevant and satisfactory secondary education for primary school leavers for whom there is no opportunity to go to high school.'[46] The intention to 'promote personal development and practical experience' was (again) well meant; but it was not what the pupils and their parents wanted.[47] Hence the incorporation of the CSE ethos into the 'regular' academic curriculum of the high school, in 1977. In effect, the 'cooling out' would be deferred, from Grade 6 to Grade 8. Popular demand for high school education would be satisfied; but a truly academic education would be reserved for those students who managed to squeeze through the narrow entrance doors into Grades 9 and 10. This, at any rate, was the theory behind the reform. In practice, it could be – and in fact was – only a matter of time before CSEP was succeeded by SSCEP (see Chapter Seven), a project that would integrate the academic and practical components of a 'secondary education for all'.

References

[1]Beltz, C. L., 'High level manpower: current situation and future prospects', in New Guinea Research Unit (1970), p. 112.
[2]ibid.
[3]Sheehan, Barry A., 'The vanishing school', in Thomas (1976), p. 86.
[4]White (1965, revised 1972), p. 219.
[5]Oram (1976), p. 116.
[6]Nelson (1974), p. 175.
[7]Conroy, John, 'Dilemmas of educational policy', in Clunies-Ross and Langmore (1973), p. 141.
[8]Rowley (1965), p. 201.
[9]Clarke (1975), p. 325.

[10]Brown (1973), p. 97.

[11]Morauta (1974), p. 153.

[12]Matane (1972), p. 103.

[13]Kiki (1968), pp. 110–11.

[14]Diro, Ted, in Steinbauer (1974), p. 81.

[15]Hihina, John Banono, in ibid., p. 76.

[16]Kiki (1968), p. 111.

[17]Oliver (1973), p. 152.

[18]ibid., p. 154.

[19]ibid., p. 169.

[20]Hastings (1973), p. 191.

[21]Epstein (1969), pp. 283, 286.

[22]Palmer (1978), pp. 9, 40.

[23]Todd (1974), p. 46.

[24]Lawrence, P., 'European cultism: the skeleton in the scientific cupboard', in Brammall and May (1975), p. 341.

[25]Woolford (1976), p. 11.

[26]Morauta (1974), pp. 40, 102.

[27]Harding, T. G., and Lawrence, P., 'Cash crops or cargo?' in Epstein *et al.* (1971), pp. 181, 182.

[28]ibid., p. 199; Hastings (1973), p. 137; Nelson (1974), p. 132.

[29]Epstein *et al.* (1971), p. 171.

[30]Clarke (1975), pp. 21, 231.

[31]Nelson (1974), p. 132.

[32]ibid., p. 136.

[33]Harding, T. G. & Lawrence, P., 'Cash crops or cargo?' in Epstein *et al.* (1971), p. 213.

[34]Somare (1975), p. 84.

[35]Todd (1974), p. 107.

[36]Clarke (1975), p. 116.

[37]Hastings (1973), p. 30.

[38]Morauta (1974), p. 163.

[39]Somare (1975), p. 54.

[40]Woolford (1976), p. 236.

[41]McKinnon, K. R., 'Priorities in education in Papua New Guinea' in Thomas (1976), p. 196.

[42]Kaputin, John, 'Same education needed to reach the village or the Moon' in Weeks (1976), p. 159.

[43]Department of Education (1978), p. 11.

[44]ibid.

[45]ibid., p. 13.

[46]Silachot, Emmanuel & Kemelfield, Graeme, 'Community secondary education project: an innovation in further education for primary school leavers' in Department of Education (1979), p. 20.

[47]ibid., p. 22.

7

Disenchantment

Part One. The town

The cargoism of the first gabbling, prophesying, marching and mimicking cults became the cargoism of the political groups working for (and against) self-government. Symbols changed over time, from baptism, through the Bible, singing, prayer, literacy in English, primary schooling, high school education, community development, cash-cropping, copper-mining, and local councils, to voting, and party membership, and independence. What Worsley calls the 'transition from magical to political action',[1] was essentially an evolution from a lesser to a greater rationality. Put another way, it was a progressive shift from indigenous, to European norms of perception and behaviour. The Europeans and their schools, and stores, and House of Assembly had come to stay. Cultural imperialism had worked its effects for good and ill, and there was no holding out against it. Each new promise, each new symbol was accepted, believed in, and acted upon, at first enthusiastically, then empirically, and at last sceptically. Stent summarises the general attitude towards the promises and symbols, in the pidgin phrase 'mi traim tasol' (it's worth a try).[2] Cult movements came and went. Cult leaders named dates for the arrival of cargo, and so gave hostages to fortune. Villagers had grown accustomed to unfulfilled promises: 'They could recall promises of wealth by the mystical multiplication of money buried in an ancestral graveyard, by the arrival of aeroplanes stuffed with valuables . . . and by the sudden beaching of huge fish disgorging money after being trapped on river shoals following a great flood.'[3]

Yet (Downs agrees with Worsley), to believe in such wonders, to build dummy wharves, to search the river banks, and to line the beaches were perfectly rational acts in a context of ignorance and inequity. As knowledge grew, so did scepticism; and each cult movement was less of an act of desperation than its predecessor. At the same time, though cargoism came to be less and less overt (by common consent, less cargo was promised in the 1968 elections than in those of 1964),[4] the hopes reposed in successive rounds of cult activity did not diminish by one item the shopping list of material wants. Seifert interviewed 'the man in the street' to find out what he spent his money on. One reply (made on behalf of a circle of relatives) was as follows:

> regular items like food, tobacco, and soap; a lot of clothes, mostly shirts, and trousers or shorts; some blankets, sheets, pillows, and mattresses; plates, saucepans, frypans, teapots, and eating utensils; safety razors, shave cream, hair oil and toothpaste; a mirror, a padlock, a bicycle, a radio, a kerosene stove, a torch and an axe; also some phonograph records, some tools, some traditional decorations for when there is a big celebration . . . and finally a machine for husking coffee beans.[5]

The man in the street was by no means tongue-tied when he was asked what he wanted in life. His wants had not altered (they had been enlarged by developments, if anything) – only the means by which he imagined they might be satisfied had changed. He had abandoned Christianity when it failed to deliver material goods: Lawrence refers to the reversion to paganism of the Ngaing people, when they lost faith in the wealth-creating powers of the new religion;[6] and Todd gives an account of a similar disillusionment with Christianity, and defection from it, among the Tolai of the Gazelle Peninsula.[7] He had abandoned local government councils when these disappointed. Morauta speaks of 'considerable apathy' among the voters and tax payers of Ambenob, Madang; then she re-interprets the thirty-eight per cent turnout at the 1969 elections, as 'dissatisfaction' rather than mere apathy.[8] Yali registered disgust at what he took to be the perfidy of white promise-makers, and Yaliwan was as unimpressed by the House of Assembly, as he was unimpressive in it. Disillusionment with European institutions was cumulative and insidious. It would have been a marvel if schools had been spared customer resistance, they had been oversold so grossly for so long.

Entry to grade one was the thin end of a widening wedge. By the time a child reached Grade 6, (s)he had one foot already in the white man's world. William Conton (born in the Gambia, and educated in Sierra Leone) speaks of his sadness in the face of a simple truth: 'I realised, with feelings of embarrassment that already, before even entering secondary school, I had learned much more than either of my parents ever had or would; and that this fact, which might appear now superficially to be closing the gap between my father and me, was in fact widening it in every important respect.'[9] As in Gambia, and Sierra Leone, so in New Guinea, to go to school was to grow away from home. 'The syllabus in the Primary School seems to be written with the urban child in mind. Therefore the urban child has a great advantage over the rural child.' So wrote Bishop Ashton, in 1977.[10] And he was right; the syllabus had the urban child in mind because it was the urban child who stood on street corners and begged, and hawked, and was an embarrassment. And a syllabus that took account of the special needs of the rural child, would not have been tolerated by rural parents. Had there been such discrimination, villagers would then have agreed with Bishop Ashton that the urban child had a 'great advantage' over his rural age-mate. Nothing else would have satisfied them than a schooling which gave village children the chance to compete for jobs in town. They knew that there were such jobs because they heard about life in town on the radio; the radio was the voice of the town in the village, and it was a remote village indeed that was without a single receiver tuned to one or another Pidgin – or Motu-speaking station. But then, it was a remote village that was without a road of some sort, suitable for four-wheel drive Land Cruisers; and this road would lead to another road, which led to a town.

The growing familiarity bred discontent. Director of Education Mr McNamara was only too conscious of the position in which village school children were placed: 'If they try really hard to reject traditional life and embrace the new way of life of the school, they will get into high school. So they all try very hard indeed to fit themselves for town.'[11] Like the radio, the primary school was the

voice of the town in the very heart of the village. The teacher was
an outsider with an income that shut all others out of his house and
his life. He had no need to grow his own vegetables, or do work of
a do-it-yourself sort. He presented a clean-handed role-model to
his pupils;[12] indeed, inasmuch as he would probably have been
happier in an urban school, he transmitted to his pupils a quite
inappopriate distaste of the bush and the backwoods. The teacher
was an alien, the school building was alien, the language was alien,
and the standard of living was attractive to a degree. If there was
one pupil who did not want to wear smart clothes and have clean
hands, he was the exception who proved the rule.

> 'Your clothes are smart.'
> 'Yes. Well, that is it.'
> 'Aren't you living in the village any more?'
> 'Nuh, man. I done wid the village long time. That is foolishness there
> boy. What I have to do wid cutting cane an' min'ing cow like a fool! I
> done wid that.'[13]

The accent is Caribbean; but boys in Papua had no more taste for
playing the fool than boys in the Trinidad of Ian McDonald's novel
The Humming-Bird Tree. There were, at the same time, certain
losses of which even determined schoolboys were forced to take
account. New Guinean Siump Kavani ran away to school against
the wishes of the village elders. He went thinking he would 'enjoy
the strange pleasure of being a schoolboy', just for a short time; but
he did not find the experience enjoyable:

> Then, in 1962, an *Ifoba'ne* ceremony was announced for my age-group.
> I rejoiced. I thought I would at last be released from school, that I
> would go through the ceremony and pass into adulthood from my
> growing years. But instead I was told that as I was going to school to
> understand the white man, I would not be initiated . . . With a terrible
> shock I suddenly realised that time and effort had been wasted on me by
> clan elders. That without initiation I would never be considered a man
> amongst my own people and that I had in fact become a drop-out.[14]

Nelson Giraure of East New Britain was another drop-out from
the village. Not only was he not taught the myths and legends of
his ancestors; not only did he not join in the dances and ceremonies
of his village; he – whose house was no more than 20 metres from
the sea, whose people had always been fishermen – grew up (as he

puts it) 'without knowing how to pull a fish in'.[15] There were those boys who, like Kavani, regretted being cut off from the tribe, who sought initiation; and there were those who underwent it out of a sense of duty, for whom it had lost much of its old meaning.

The effects of education were likely to be still more unsettling for girls than boys, since those girls who did go to school were already having to overcome native resistance to female emancipation in any shape or form. Girls had not gone to the coast to labour on the plantations, nor had they joined the patrol officer's police force; there was in short, no precedent for the advancement of girls, in a money-earning career sense. Even the mission helpers, and domestic servants in European houses were 'boys'. Frankel investigated an outbreak of mass hysteria, in the Telefomin (West Sepik) area, in 1974. Of the twenty-two women affected, twelve had had formal schooling. Frankel surmised that to have gone to school, and then to have returned to villages in which women were even more restricted than usual, was a traumatic experience for sensitive girls.[16]

It did not do to read too many books – not if convention demanded that you settle for the simple life. An educated girl would either command an inflated bride-price, or she would be deemed 'spoilt' by those who could afford to pay. What is more, it was harder for a girl to marry 'beneath' her, than it was for a boy superior from birth. It is no wonder that the PNG Education Secretary, Mr Alkan Tololo, had to report in 1978, that 'the department's goal of equal opportunity for girls was progressing painfully slowly'. The forty per cent of girls at the primary school level, fell to thirty per cent at high schools, and to twenty-three per cent in Grades 11 and 12 – and these were figures for the country as a whole; in areas of the Highlands, the ratios were lower still.[17]

Girls and boys were equally susceptible to the tensions inherent in the life of the undergraduate. Olewale has called students at U.P.N.G. 'stateless persons', such was the crisis of identity through which they passed.[18] This crisis in many cases had physical effects. Frankel relates that of 1100 students, 500 had attended the university clinic every year, up until 1976. They showed, he says, 'physical symptoms caused solely by somaticised anxiety'.[19] Undergraduates paid a high price for their room at the top. But it was the price that had been paid by students who had won scholarships to secondary schools in Australia; and it was a price only halfpence higher than that paid for an urban room half way to the top by village boys with half an education. The undergraduate had spent ten or a dozen years in the classroom, many of them in boarding schools a long way from home. They were town mice already in spirit. For country mice with no more than a Grade 6 certificate, life and work in the town might be exciting, or harrowing. There were those who sank, and those who swam.

Young people migrated to the towns for negative and positive reasons. Vambe describes the migration, as he observed it in what was then, Southern Rhodesia:

> By far the most significant movement among young educated Chishawasha was that away from the traditional environment, in which men and women had once lived practically all their lives, to Salisbury and beyond. Once the average boy had done his stint at school, inevitably the tribe was too narrow and sterile for him; it was as if he had been deliberately poisoned by it.[20]

The conventional view is that the young were attracted to the city's 'bright lights'. There were those who calculated that the chances of completing their education were greater in the town than in the village.[21] There were those who were attracted by the variety of town life, and by the range of services available there. And there were those who sought a better material existence, even when there was no more than half a chance that they would survive in the city, let alone thrive.[22] Schooling opened the eyes of pupils not merely to the positive aspects of life in towns – the bars, the cinema, the shops, the jobs and all that money could buy; it also opened them to the negative aspects of life in the village. First among these was the hostile attitude of parents and relatives towards those pupils (the majority) who, after six or eight years of fee-paid schooling, failed to gain a place at a high school, or in Grade 9 of the high school course. Such students were stigmatised as failures unless they found a job that would enable them to repay every shilling of what their sponsors had invested in them. Migration to the town served as a means of evading the accusing eye, and of earning enough to honour debts.

But not only money was invested in the young. Clan leaders had suffered a loss of pride and dignity in the face of the obviously superior white man. Only one means offered itself by which self-respect might be restored, and that was by seeking equality with him, on his own terms, in the classroom, and the white-collar job market. When children failed to be admitted to high school, their families heaped their bitter disappointment on their heads, and drove them out.[23] But then, even where families were more forgiving, and could give employment of a sort to hands willing to work, few Grade 6 leavers could settle for the humble satisfaction to be got from subsistence farming. They had outgrown old forms of social control; they could no longer defer unthinkingly to fathers and elders; and they could no longer give unstinting friendship to unschooled peers. Furthermore, life in the village could be decidedly dull, fit only for 'bush kanakas' and 'rubbish men'. What the patrol officers had not banned – head-hunting, and clan fighting – the missionaries disapproved of, and inhibited. The Lutheran mission disparaged dancing and bodily decoration;[24] singsings and other celebrations inseparable from ancestor-worship, were falling into disuse and disrespect. Excitement went the way of savagery, and all that was left was void.

Even if school-leavers had wanted to return to the land, there would not invariably have been land enough to support them. Their fathers and mothers were living longer, and fewer of their brothers and sisters died in infancy. It has been calculated that in some areas, European medicine and health education had made for a seventy per cent increase in population, over one or two generations.[25] The shortage of land could be a potent factor in the decision to migrate to the town. Another was the ever-present fear of sorcery; six years in a white man's schools were small guarantee against a fear that ran as deep as that of the sorcerer's evil eye.[26] But its gleam might be annulled by bright lights.

'I came out here raw and proud the way you are,' Maina said to Meja scraping away the rotten side of an orange. 'I thought I would get a job and earn six–seven hundred shillings a month. Then I would get a house, a radio, good clothes and food.' He paused . . .
'Well I tried to get a job,' he said and shrugged. '"What qualifications?" they would ask me. "Second Division School Cert . . ." I would start to say, but before I had finished the man behind the desk would roar, "Get out, we have no jobs."'[27]

The city is Nairobi, and the two tramps are young Kenyans; but it could as well be Port Moresby. Many young New Guineans with high hopes were reduced to scraping the rotten sides of oranges. There were 10,000 students in Grade 8 classes in 1976. These represented thirty per cent of the students – who had attended Grade 6 classes in 1974 (themselves the survivors of several annual prunings). Yet even at this rate of attrition, there were too few job-openings for those who stayed the full ten-year course; therefore, only sixty per cent (6,000) of the Grade 8 students would be allowed to advance into the second cycle of secondary education, and so to the Grade 10 school-leaving examinations. One high school headmaster, at least, asked whether the remaining forty per cent of 'school-leavers' were a 'satisfied, grateful group'. His finding was that they were not: '. . . the vast majority are unhappy, resentful, confused and frustrated.'[28]

Three years before (in 1973), and two years before independence, Conroy had expressed the fear that 'push-outs' from the secondary schools would be a more serious threat to public order than primary school leavers. Their presence in growing numbers in the towns of Papua New Guinea, said Conroy, could have 'politically destabilising consequences'.[29] To those with an interest in the preservation of the status quo, groups of alienated youths, unemployed, and 'resentful', would certainly have appeared menacing. But it was already too late to agonise about the political effects of urban unemployment: of greater moment in the long run, were its social and moral effects on life in the towns, and on the luckless youths themselves. Strathern has typified the psycho-pathology of the rootless ones in these terms: 'urban migrants are able to pursue a style of life which has a strong adolescent flavour . . . What there does not seem to be is any ethic of maturity.'[30] They were not all youths by any means, these migrants, but they behaved as if they were. They were refugees from the authority structure of the village, and of the school; they lived like poor men at the gates of the white man's castle, and despaired of getting in. Deprived of job chances without access to political power, schooled to be scavengers, and revenge-takers by the clan, they were natural candidates for crime. They had wanted, and expected, to earn money, so that they could live in houses, of steel, wood and fibre; run cars, and drink beer, and wear blue jeans; go to cinemas and barbecues like Australians, buy records, and play pool. There were so many things the migrants had looked forward to buying and doing, but the nearest most black men could get to this sort of action, was to watch white men playing all the leading roles. On a set where white men did the casting and directing and producing, black men could never be more than extras, paid pocket-money by the day. The Europeans drove air-conditioned cars, sent servants to the supermarket, and lived in stilted houses with guard dogs, behind chain-link fences and palms. Rowley stated the case in these words: 'The desperate economic situation of many leads to theft and burglary. Marginal Man may be found by neither town nor village morality . . . Contrast of his lot with that of the whites makes their homes and possessions appear fair game.'[31]

That was twenty years ago. During that time, the number of 'marginal men' has grown out of all proportion to the growth in the number of jobs. The first migrants could always lodge with their 'wantoks' (one-talks) – members of the clan, the village, or the extended family, who had made the move some time before, and who rented a room, or lived in a boy-house. An obligation to extend hospitality to wantoks was assumed. The relationship might be a tenuous one, but when two Chimbus from the same language-group were thrown together hundreds of miles away, no stronger bond was needed. As Ryan says, it was no 'mystic compulsion' that prompted those already in town to give space for a sleeping-mat to wantoks from the bush; it was self-interest.[32] None could tell when he would be compelled to turn to others for help and hospitality; 'wantokism' was friendly society, welfare system, and life-assurance all in one. The urban worker from the East Sepik still thought of his village as home. Port Moresby was home only to those in the fishing villages – Koki and Hanuabada – absorbed by what came to be called the Capital District. When the Sepik villager went home on leave, he did not return to a garden of his own, yielding food to last his stay. He relied on the good offices of those to whom he had afforded food in town, or who had heard it reported that he had fed others.[33] Exchange theory was still very much the practice – that is, until the trickle of immigrants became a flood. Then, the exchange principle broke down, because the relationship came to be too one-sided. The urban worker (if he was fortunate enough to be in work) had to learn how to refuse to be the host to hangers-on whose stay might be indefinite, and whose demands never-ending. If self-interest had called for generosity before, it called for prudence now. The extended family system had been acceptable, as Gunton says, in 'conditions of more or less uniform poverty';[34] in the urban context, (when possession of a few items of furniture or clothing made the possessor look rich) the wage earner and the unemployed could no longer share and share alike. The former might try to be faithful to the old canons of exchange – perhaps in fear of the consequences if he did not; he might beggar himself in the process. But if he had a family of his own, he soon discovered that, just as traditional exchange relationships could not be reconciled with capitalist individualism, so the interests of the clan did not often coincide with those of the urban nuclear family. The urban wage earner was both victim and priest of a changing social–economic structure that he could neither understand nor manage. When it appeared to the migrants that the new ways were failing them, they not infrequently reverted to the old. What could not be acquired by legal, peaceful means, would have to be taken by force.

Cargo activity had been the fruit of cultural confusion before; crime was its counterpart now. In recent years, the Port Moresby daily newspaper, the Post–Courier, has contained articles about the 'crime wave', letters from the victims of crime, and weekly totals of 'break-and-enter' offences notified in the Capital District. From time to time one letter in particular will stimulate a flood of correspondence from the aggrieved and fearful. The following is an extract from such a letter:

> Dear Sir,
>
> I am writing this letter at 4.30 a.m. The police have just left our house and with several very important exceptions everything is settling down to a normal state for this house in the morning.
>
> The exceptions are my wife and children – a girl aged three-and-a-half years and a boy aged three-and-a-half months.
>
> My son is crying.
>
> His mother has only been able to give him one breast full of milk because the other breast is badly bruised and painful.
>
> It was struck by a large rock hurled at her through our kitchen window about an hour ago by an escaping intruder.
>
> Several things are missing – K25 in cash and a transistor radio, but I am too disgusted to do a proper check.

Last time it was most of our cooking utensils and tape recordings.

The time before that, my daughter was thrown from her cot to the floor . . . The time before that, all my clothes were stolen and so on.

Our neighbours can relate similar experiences . . . I have been in Papua New Guinea with the Public Service for the best part of twelve years and have worked hard for what I regarded as a worthwhile cause.

We now want to leave as soon as possible for a number of reasons, the main one being that we can never again look forward to a night's rest in the 'security' of our 'home' . . .

ONE OF THE MANY
Lawes Road[35]

Primary education, at least, was near-universal in the capital, in the interests of containment; and several authorities have argued that preference should be given to urban areas, in plans for the development of secondary education, in light of the fact that young people in towns were no longer occupied by the traditional routines of rural life.[36] Within days of the publication of the above letter, Mr Somare, the Prime Minister, announced measures designed to combat urban crime. These measures were welcomed by the M.H.A. for Moresby South, Mr Sevese Morea; but, he said, Mr Somare was not going to the root of the problem. In his speech to Parliament, Mr Morea said:

The root of the problem is the class society we have built. We have built an environment that is conducive to crime. Our youths go to school, leave at standard six either because they failed or because there was not enough space in high schools, and they find themselves rejected by society.

The youth in the rural area has his garden and hunting to keep him occupied, but our youths in the urban areas like Port Moresby, Lae and Rabaul have nothing to occupy themselves with.

They try to get jobs but they are turned away because they are not old enough. They try to get further education but they are considered too old.

Ultimately, they end up back in the bedbug ridden houses they grew up in and they become derelicts of society . . .

Brother, if you are hungry and you have no dough in your pocket, you're going to steal.[37]

Many of those who did not steal – whether out of scruple, or a lack of enterprise, or fear of the police – turned to beer, or to gambling. The Melanesian had known nothing of fermented liquor before the

white man came. Fruit and vegetables grew in abundance, yet he
had not produced a beer, a wine, or a spirit from any of them,
either by accident or design. The white man came with all three of
these potions, but he was in no mind to share them with the
uninitiated. Until November 1962, Papua New Guineans were
forbidden to consume alcoholic liquor of any sort, on any
premises.[38] Hoiri (in Eri's *The Crocodile*) gazes through the window
of a Port Moresby liquor store, with a more knowledgeable
wantok:

> Hoiri pointed to bottles of different shapes and sizes behind the wire in a
> locked cupboard. Some of them were ideal for keeping water in to take
> to the gardens. 'Can we buy the tall one with the fat base?' he asked.
> 'No we can't. All those are the bad water that the white men and
> women drink when they are tired. Do you remember the night when
> the *taubada* and *sinabada* had a party? When they drank that water, they
> talk like small children and their eyes do not see very well.'
> 'But why can't we drink that water too?'
> 'Well, the white people are afraid: they are afraid we will become clever
> like them and make these different things that you see on the shelves.'[39]

What the white people were really afraid of, of course, was that the
black people would become intoxicated, and misbehave. The
natives were restless enough as they were; to give them liquor
would be asking for trouble.

There were those, after November 1962 who said: 'I told you
so'. Chewing betel-nut had induced pleasant sensations; but the
effects of beer were still more interesting, more rapid, and less
messy. To those who had never tasted it before, beer was a
revelation. To those who had tasted it, it came to be one of the
reasons for being. On alternate Fridays, the beer shops filled with
customers, and the dustbins filled with cans. Broken beer bottles
littered yards, and alternate Mondays were the mornings after the
nights before. Beer drinking in Papua New Guinea was good for
the brewers, but otherwise – at least in the short term – losses
outweighed gains. Where there was frustration, beer lent amnesia;
where there was boredom, and colourlessness, the cinema provided
an escape.

Card playing, and the gambling that went with it, were another
much used escape route. But these were not new. Hogbin, in 1951,
described gambling as the 'chief pastime' for the hours of idleness

on the labour-line. The men played 'Lucky' – and some were, winning several pounds in a night. Others mortgaged their earnings for some months ahead before they would admit defeat.[40] A 'man in the street' confessed all to Seifert: 'We like to spend money in card games. Part of the attraction is that card playing is looked on as a form of "earning" money.'[41] There is some evidence, indeed, that the old belief in sympathetic magic still operated: as money rubbed against money, it was believed, it would reproduce itself before the gamblers' very eyes.[42] A chain-letter racket took hold of the Maprik sub-district in the early 1970s, in much the same spirit. Australian Bonanza, as it was called, was run from Sydney; the postal system must have done as well out of the affair as its organisers, until the Administration banned mail associated with it, in 1973. The people of Maprik did not know what to make of the ban: either the whole thing had been a fraud, or they had been on to something, and the white man had blocked the road as he had always done before.[43] It was all very vexing and mysterious. But no ban fell on winning and losing at cards; this has continued to be something more than a pastime – it has become a compelling ritual, calling devotees to cargo prayer thrice daily.

Part Two. The school

Schools, and the school system, have had to re-consider the job that they are doing. As the number of 'failures' has grown, the schools have had to give serious thought to what part they themselves have played in the failure to meet the needs of all but a minority of their clients. The headmaster of St Xavier's High School, Wewak, admitted in 1975: 'For many years now we have been unhappy with the number of our students who have failed to cope with the world beyond the school and have felt that our training here was at least a part of the fault.' He held discussions with ex-pupils of the school, and concluded that among the problems to be faced were 'unrealistic expectations', and 'a cargo mentality towards edu-cation'.[44] However valid these conclusions might be, it is doubtful whether they can have led to measures that would enable greater numbers of students to cope with the world beyond the school. The problems were greater than it lay within the competence of any one school to solve.

Michael Wilson also held discussions with ex-pupils, at Tambul, in the Western Highlands, and in the Kara sub-district of New Ireland. He asked them the very specific question, whether any of the things that they had learnt at school had been a waste of time. Though almost all the school-leavers expressed satisfaction that they had been to school (because they had learnt to speak and read and write in English), only thirty-three per cent of the Tambul students could think of anything that had been a 'waste of time', whilst fifty-two per cent of the Kara students produced 'a long list of subjects which they considered fell into this category'. The irony is that, of the two groups of students, it was the Tambul students who saw education in the more 'cargo cultist' terms. The white man and his schools had been in New Ireland over a much longer period, therefore schooling was understood in more realistic terms, and its 'long term effects (were) better known'.[45] Wilson does not spell it out, but he might have used Keating's description of these effects of the failure of the school system to cater for the ten per cent of the Grade 6 intake, and the further forty per cent of the Grade 8 intake, refused access respectively to Grades 7 and 9: unhappiness, resentment, confusion, and frustration.

Yet these were intermediate effects; one long-range, very direct effect was parental withdrawal of support for the schools. To some extent, the disaffection has been analogous with the reversion from Christianity to paganism, following what was supposed to be the Church's failure to share cargo secrets with its adherents. The damage to classrooms, and threats to teachers, on Bali Island, West New Britain bore the characteristics of this reversion syndrome. A Teachers' Association officer reported that cargo cultists had tried to prevent children from attending school; they had then vented their anger on the local police station, and District Office, for good measure.[46] But the above-mentioned withdrawal of support was of a more serious kind than this mere reactionary cargoism, serious in respect of motive and consequence. There have not been wanting warnings of what might happen: Philip Foster pointed to the experience of a number of African countries, where primary school enrolments fell, in line with the fall in private rates of return from formal schooling. If, as Foster says, 'educational expansion is subject to the laws of the market place',[47] we might expect as much consumer resistance to fee-paid schooling in Melanesia, as in

Africa. Thomas Welsh predicted, in 1976, that the 'laws' would apply to Papua New Guinea according to a four-stage process: a. disillusionment with the present system, b. withdrawal of children from the schools, c. a period of waiting and evaluation, and d. renewed participation in education as the result of land over-crowding and the diminution of rural food production.[48] There is much to suggest that the second stage is well underway. When the news and views in the national press do not relate to urban crime, (or to the venality of MHA's and local councillors), they fasten on public disenchantment with the schools:

School Starters Drop
Few children are starting school in East New Britain and authorities are worried.
The Superintendent of schools in ENB, Mr John Hereman, predicted last week that the problem of illiteracy would worsen if boards and management and parents did not encourage more enrolments.
(Post–Courier, 6.6.78)

Lack of Support – School Closes
Lack of support from parents had forced the closure of a community school near Lae, Morobe Province.
The school superintendent in the Morobe Province, Mr Alan Isoaimo, said the Lalou Miti Community School had been closed because of lack of parental support.
(Hailans Nius, 15.5.78)

'No One Thinks it Matters'
Education is not considered as important today as it was ten years ago, a committee looking into the standard of education in East New Britain says.
The committee remarked on 'the apparent casualness on everyone's behalf' towards education.
(Post–Courier, 11.12.79)

Wastage: 'Closure of Schools No Answer'
Threatening to close schools if parents did not make their children attend would not solve the problem of wastage, a teachers' represen-tative said.

But parents had other ways of forcing the authorities to close schools than not sending their children to them, as this report shows:

Three Schools Close
Three community schools in the Duke of York Islands, East New Britain, were closed last week . . . The Education Services Committee

. . . acted because the villagers had failed to build adequate toilet
facilities at the school and for the teachers' houses.

(Post–Courier, 6.11.79)

And these were the new-look primary schools that the public was
neglecting – not the high schools for the minority; not the national
high schools for the élite. These were the community schools,
newly named and boosted by the five-year plan for 1977–82. These
were the schools that were designed to attract eighty-six per cent of
the child population of school age, by 1981; the schools that would
encourage eighty-three per cent of grade one entrants to stay the
course to Grade 6; the schools that would express the government's
determination to revoke the policy of the 1960s (with its emphasis
on the development of education at the secondary and tertiary
levels) in favour of Hasluck's universal primary education policy of
the 1950s. The community schools were to supply the country's
'basic education needs'. They were to teach nationals the sort of
development skills for lack of which PNG was more dependent on
foreign aid than any other 'developing' country.[49] Yet, in February
1978, the *Post–Courier* newspaper gave page-one headlines to the
following report:

> *Millions Lost on Dropouts*
> Millions of kina are being wasted each year because of the number of
> children who drop out of community schools. In some cases, only 50 to
> 60 pupils out of 100 starting grade one reach grade six.
> Disclosing this yesterday, the education Minister, Mr Tammur, said he
> was shocked at the size of the problem . . .
> Wastage was so high that the Education Department did not expect to
> reach the 1980 enrolment targets set in the five-year plan.
> 'In terms of the population being educated, the country has taken a step
> backwards'.   (*Post–Courier*, 2.2.78)

We have seen something of the reasoning behind the popular
rejection of vocational schooling (see above, Chapter Four). The
Community Secondary Education Project was billed as an 'innovation in further education for primary school-leavers'. It was,
strictly speaking, pre-vocational, in that school-leavers too young
to enter employment or (the rather few) vocational centres, were
given encouragement to take simple, business initiatives of a self-
help kind. What was proposed was an 'all-round scheme of

activities comprising academic, vocational, cultural, sports, and community service components'.[50] Parents were interested in the project as long as the academic component was to the fore; that it took three years for their sons and daughters to reach a standard equivalent to Grade 8, instead of two, was no great loss. What forfeited public interest in the scheme was: 'insufficient initial consultation with communities, leading to a failure on the part of parents to understand the purpose of the scheme. Support (was) withdrawn when the academic studies component (was) not seen to offer the reward of high school entrance.'[51]

It did not help the new secondary schools that they were said to purvey 'community' secondary education; and it did not help the new primaries that they were called 'community' schools. The community did not wish to be put in its place; to be told what was good and sufficient for it; to be shown a road that turned back on itself – away from all that had seemed to make an arduous journey worthwhile. Village people sensed betrayal, and when school fees were raised in January 1979, they threatened revolt.[52] Parents did not question what their children did in Grade one, so long as it led to Grade two; they did not begrudge the payment of fees for primary schooling, until they saw the road to secondary schooling narrow to a strait gate. Each examination was a rite of passage; each grade was a milepost on the road that had meaning only for those who made it to the end. What was vital, if the community was to accept its 'community' school, was evidence that Grade 6 leavers (hitherto regarded as 'drop-outs' and 'failures') had something of real value to contribute to the life and work of the village.[53] All too often, the evidence was all the other way. A research investigation into 'youth in their villages' found that – whilst many school-leavers retained skills learnt at school, to their own personal satisfaction – parents did not find that those who had been to school were more useful to them than those who had not. Indeed, school had made the schooled 'too lazy to co-operate with their parents'; and those who did migrate to the town 'only maximised their own welfare'.[54]

Many PNG village elders must have felt with the Kenyan elders of Jako's tribe (in *The Villager's Son* by Asenath Odaga), that a boy sent to school would not do hard work on his return; and they said as much to his father: 'If this boy is sent to the white man's school,

do you think when he returns he will still want to cut and chop
wood and carve statues and the like in the manner you have done?
This is the main reason why we disagree with you. Instead of
sending him to school, we would rather he stayed here and learned
from you.'[55]

Community schools were, by definition, not boarding schools.
Children were six years old (at least) before they entered them, and
they might not stay long. White expatriates were gradually being
replaced by indigenous teachers who may well have had no more
than eight years of formal schooling. It goes without saying that
European teachers had 'nothing in common with the community',[56] but indigenous teachers were more often than not
strangers, too. Just as policemen were posted to stations away from
their own 'wantoks' in the interests of discipline, and mutual
respect, so teachers were directed to schools where there could be
no hint of influence, favouritism, or bad blood. Such teachers were
often young, and uncertain of themselves. They might well not
understand their host communities, and be misunderstood. It only
needed parents to withdraw their children, for one reason or
another, and for enrolments to fall, for the teachers' morale to fall
in proportion. All the conditions were then present for the sort of
teacher-absenteeism, and inefficiency complained of in ministry
circulars of the late 1970s.[57] The school day was foreshortened, less
time was given to English and arithmetic (in which the teacher
might be deficient), breaks and lunchtimes were extended by
default, and pupils missed classes with impunity. The stage was set
for letters to the press about declining standards, such as this one
from Mr G. Yerua, of Keravat, East New Britain:

> At the moment, many of you are criticising the Education Department
> because the standard of education children get at school is very low, in
> contrast to other countries.
> Many of you complain that national teachers do not teach your children
> properly. I strongly support your criticism of the Education Depart-
> ment, but not our poor teachers.
> Our teachers are doing their best up to their ability to teach our children
> with the knowledge they gained from teachers' colleges . . .
> In the long run, if we want to produce brainy young Papua New
> Guineans for our country, then we need well qualified national teachers
> . . .[58]

'European' education that was short and unsatisfactory soon succumbed to the old learning, like a road reverting to bush. It did not take long for the chanting of verbs and tables, the reading of symbols, and the painful writing of letters to look about as relevant to farming and fishing as drilling with bamboo guns. The new knowledge and value-system (for which the teachers themselves were often unconvincing spokesmen) could be discarded with as little scruple as shoes and stockings.

But it must not be supposed that all school-leavers were equally enamoured of (the prospect of) life in the town. Nor were all parents equally opposed to the philosophy of community schooling. Wilson's (rural) Tambul parents expected their children to seek wage employment when they left school, and this inevitably meant leaving the village. Kara parents on the other hand, were content for their children to remain at home because access by road to Kavieng meant that there were wage earning opportunities within easy commuting distance of the coastal villages.[59] It was less often a question of whether it was better to live in a town or a village *per se*, than of the relative possibilities of earning cash. These were generally greater in the town, but where there was paid work to be had in the provinces, this was often the preferred alternative to the hazard of the unknown in town. Conroy, Oram, Wilson, and Weeks all make this point after independent research in different parts of the country.[60] Thomas quotes the finding of Conroy and Stent, who asked the question, 'Would it be better for young people to stay in the village if they could earn money there?', of three communities in the Highlands. An almost uniform eighty per cent of responses were in the affirmative.[61] This consensus, however (of both researchers and researched) does not alter two testing truths: firstly, there is no less agreement that the opportunities for wage earning in the villages are decidedly restricted; and secondly (as we have seen) those young people who have been to school are no better placed to start small businesses than those who have not. Robert Paia puts it plainly thus:

> I found that education is not an investment for the youth who stay in the village. Youths with no education are more productive in the village. We tend to think that education is the only key to the businesses, which is not true. Non-schooled youths observe what is happening around them and select the best way they can find and then

practise it themselves on a small scale till they acquire more knowledge and experience . . . many of the jobs which the young people do in the villages demand skills that are not learned in school.[62]

If an 'academic' education counted for little in the subsistence world of the village, it counted for little more in the cash economy of the town. Neither church nor state gave a moral lead to replace that of the elders back home. That no fewer than thirty-seven independent Christian evangelical organisations were competing for souls in the early 'seventies left the more thoughtful more thoughtful still.[63] And the aid said to be flowing into the country for the benefit of the native 'Niuginians' seemed, like a boomerang, to return whence it came. Australia allocated half its total foreign aid budget to PNG in the 1970s, yet little enough of this seemed to find its way into the pockets and purses of Niuginians. The number of expatriates in the country doubled between 1965 and 1975 (not all of them Australians to be sure). These expats, 'experts', had pockets and purses that never emptied; they outlawed the sale of beer by the bottle to cut native consumption – yet they bought it by the case of twenty-four themselves. (And so, as it turned out, did the natives. Whole villages clubbed together to buy in bulk and consumption increased.) They funded business enterprises, and they managed them; they built hotels for foreign experts and tourists to stay in, and they dressed native 'boys' in colourful laplaps to wait at table. Niuginians earned money; but its colour would not buy on payday what the white man's money bought morning noon and night every blessed day of the week. If there are few who now believe in a literal re-labelling of the cargo destined for the native of PNG, there are many who believe in a conspiracy to deprive them of their due. It is a suspicion not entirely without foundation, if a simple, but not simplistic, construction is placed on 'aid'.[64]

In the run up to independence, the numbers of expatriates in the positions of power, and their conspicuous consumption, fomented an obvious – though most often suppressed – resentment. The malaise of helplessness was endemic. It issued in petty crime, gambling, drinking, and withdrawal. Juveniles flouted the law most openly, leaving the (undoubted) alienation of their elders to be guessed at. Oram refers to the 'widespread feeling of insecurity' among 'all races' in Port Moresby, and to the fear of going 'abroad at night';[65] and Standish points to resentment as the origin of the 'stoning of vehicles and other harassment' to which urban whites were often subject.[66] Such anomie gave rise to doubts as to whether the police would cope, and whether the lives of white expatriates would be safe. (There was even wild talk of a Melanesian-style Mau Mau terrorism, and of post-independence 'payback'). Others argued that like dangers would mount if the country was *not* granted independence – and soon.

Native parents faced something of an analogy of this dilemma with respect to sending their children to school. Education had seemed to be the one sure way of raising the status of the black man to that of the white; now it seemed to make little difference. In a word, schooling was a gamble. When education was expensive, costs and benefits might be finely balanced.

When the likely outcome of primary schooling was secondary schooling, and a job, parents were willing to pay the price, but as the odds increased, they hesitated. In the fifteen years between 1955 and 1970 alone, the proportion of children entering high school dropped from 67 per cent, to 37 per cent. (The five-year plan published in 1975 reduced the percentage still further, to twelve per cent. Even these odds, Welsh believes, are 'not so bad that people will desist from gambling'.)[67] And the risk element was heightened by the lottery of school type. There had been speculation about the effect on examination results of attendance at a government or church school, a girls', boys' or mixed school, or an urban or rural school. Figures and folklore vied or combined to 'prove' that one sort of school was better than others when it came to delivering goods on examination day. Then Jonathan Silvey published the results of a survey of twenty-four schools, and 1769 Grade 10 students: aside from his finding that 'girls benefit from an urban school environment in general, and particularly from the kind of environment that church schools in urban areas provide',[68] the impression of variable quality was confirmed. Success in the mid-year rating examinations appeared to hang upon the luck of the draw.

The reform of the primary schools was necessary and overdue. It was high time that elementary schooling ('for all') should cease to be thought of as primary, leading to secondary, but rather be understood as complete in itself; for this is how it was for the growing majority of children. It was time, too, that this schooling was made more relevant to the life of the community from which the pupils were drawn. The fact that parents did not like the reform, because it appeared to diminish the chances of their children's upward march through ten or more grades of formal schooling, does not cast doubt on its essential right-headedness. Secondary school selection – and the secondary school curriculum – have distorted what has been offered at the elementary level for too long; and the baneful effects of the school-leaving examinations have not been significantly lessened in the 'new' community schools. Yet even these schools were still catering to the needs of only sixty-four per cent of the seven-years old population, in the late 1970s,[69] and grade one is only the first of five years of attrition. The government of newly independent PNG (a self-styled 'socialist' government) shared the democratic policy of Aluko's imaginary West African régime:

> This government is determined to abandon as an untenable anachronism the colonial policy of concentrating scarce resources on the over-luxurious education of a very small minority to the utter neglect of hundreds of thousands of other children . . .
> What was wrong with that argument? Who except a fool would not plug for the training of a hundred boys instead of one if the same amount of money would do either.[70]

Yet even if the 'scarce resources' at the government's disposal could indeed by concentrated at the elementary level, there was no guarantee that universal primary education (UPE) could be ensured in the lifetime of the contemporary crop of new-born babies – never mind that of a five-year term government. In 1973, Sheehan wrote: UPE is 'neither necessary nor feasible in PNG in the foreseeable future'.[71] Even as his ink was drying, public servants were doing their sums, and Clarke was writing this epitaph: 'It would appear that the cost of UPE in 1980 will be possibly twenty times that of the cost of educating fifty per cent of the school-age population in 1970 . . . the GNP is calculated to increase fourfold in the same period. The conclusion is that the prospects for UPE appear to be a very remote possibility.'[72]

Yet the government could not advertise the answers to their sums on bill boards beside the public highway. The 'colonial' administration of the 1950s had emphasised equity, and quantity at the primary level; its successor of the 1960s had been obliged to go for efficiency and quality at the secondary level. Was the first government of independent PNG to de-emphasise quality and quantity, in the 1970s, at both levels? No, it was not. It would make plans for expansion as became its socialist convictions. Instead of eliminating half of all primary and teachers' college places, as Lancy recommended,[73] the government simply revised school enrolment targets, and put back the date by which it hoped UPE would be achieved. In so doing it recognised that wholesale surgery of the existing system would be politically unacceptable. The government could defer expansion of the primary sector; but it could not resist the demand of parents with children already passing through grades 1–6, for an enlargement of opportunity at the secondary level. Accordingly, it allowed for the building of thirty-four new provincial high schools in the 1975 education plan, twenty-two of them by the end of 1978. In the event, ten of these were ready on schedule; and Conroy felt able to pronounce as follows: 'The Plan target for provincial high schools has been set at a lofty height; it is not now attainable – indeed, it never was'.[74] At the same time, the Provincial Government of East New Britain, the most urban, and highly developed of the provinces, was laying plans to make secondary education available right through to Grade 10, to all entrants to the system at age five. As if to steal the provincial government's clothes, the Department of Education launched a pilot Secondary School Community Extension Project (SSCEP), in 1978.

The Department had not been so disappointed by the reception given to 'community' schools at the primary level, as to avoid re-using the term in a more controlled experiment, at the secondary level. SSCEP was initiated, modestly enough, in 1978, at two high schools, Cameron High School, Milne Bay, and Manggai, New Ireland; but the aims of the Project were far-reaching. The curriculum at the SSCEP schools would be the same as at standard high schools, but it would be applied throughout to real life conditions and problems in the community. Mathematics, English, commerce, social studies, expressive arts, and science would all be taught as usual, but they would be given a practical orientation. They would be related to the needs of the coffee-buyer, the small businessman, the truck operator, and the nursery man – particularly in Grades 9 and 10. In 1979, three more schools were run on these lines for the first time, all in different provinces. The first two had proved popular with students and all their communities, because (as the acting Secretary for Education at the time admitted), 'no students in SSCEP schools were terminated at the end of grade 8'.[75] This was a very important feature of the programme. In order to win the support of parents for the scheme, SSCEP schools had to deliver the same goods as other high schools: a leaving certificate, and the chance to enter the urban employment market. In fact, they delivered goods of a demonstrably superior quality. Not only would all entrants be guaranteed a full four-year course, but they would leave with a Grade 10 certificate qualifying them to engage in economic activity as well in the village as in the town. At least one third of class time would be devoted to practical projects of the kind that the students might be expected to introduce, or develop, in their own communities: vegetable-growing, furniture-making, pineapple canning, bread-baking, cattle-raising, butterfly-culture, even crocodile breeding, according to taste, market, and ecology. Ron Stanton, the SSCEP National Co-ordinator, emphasised that the Project: 'does not force graduates to return to the village; it attempts to show them it is a viable alternative'.[76] Vulliamy goes a little further than this: one of the aims of SSCEP, he says, is 'to encourage students to think more positively about returning to the village'.[77] Since, as he adds, it is equally necessary that parents should adopt this same positive view, the balance-sheet of success and failure can be drawn up only in the long term.

The introduction of the Project would seem to have been timely. Parents had seen enough of the 'wastage' at the conventional high schools, to appreciate that if their sons and daughters had no alternative but to return to the village – even after Grade 10 – it was better that they came armed with useful skills, than that they should think village work beneath them, or that they should play the 'rascal' in town.[78] In evaluative research of the experiment at Cameron High School (and its outstation at Hihila), Vulliamy found students happy enough at the thought that they would return home 'if they failed to obtain a job'. But he reserved his judgement about the Project as a whole. The views of parents would depend ultimately, he says, on such things as: 'the school's future exam results, on the proportions of students getting jobs after grade 10, and on the attitudes and behaviour of those students not gaining such jobs.'

In a more recent paper, Vulliamy adds that it will be a significant bonus for the Project, if it can be shown that those who do enter modern-sector employment take with them the 'ideology of rural development' to which they will have been exposed.[80] This again only time will tell. At least parents will have no excuse for believing that the SSCEP schools are offering a second-best education for their students; if anything, graduates of the Project schools will have had to work a lot harder for their qualifications than the products of the unreformed high schools – especially when one considers that the latter are the sixty per cent of the Grade 8 population selected for their aptitude for 'academic' examinations. No such 'weeding' takes place in the SSCEP schools. (In fact, it should be added that many provincial governments are following the lead of the ENB Province in allowing all entrants to Grade 7, to complete four years of high school education, through to Grade 10.)[81]

There are those who have said that the development of PNG has been too rapid; and there are those who have said that it has not been rapid enough. The patronage of a Stone Age culture, by a jet age, telecommunications age culture was bound to be traumatic; but knowing reflections on the inevitability of confusion, and misunderstanding, do not help a developing country to make sense of its legacy. It is too late now to unscramble the egg. PNG may or may not be developing; but it can not now be ingnorant of what development means. Australia is close at hand, and for better or worse, is the role-model. It never could have been, nor ever can be, otherwise. Aid has bred a certain dependence, and a certain presumption that – though independent – the territory would continue to enjoy the fruits of informal membership of the federation of Australian states. But in recent years, aid has been reduced as a proportion of the national budget; and 'self-reliance' is more than a party slogan. The past is still close enough to be conserved, and sufficient numbers of people still support themselves by subsistence farming, for the option of village-based, intermediate technology to be realistic. PNG need not repeat the mistakes of those over-urbanised client-states in which the schooled and the unschooled, the city dwellers and the villagers, the haves and the have-nots stare at each other as over a fence, in mutual incomprehension, and distrust. Some quite dire warnings were issued, by expatriates and indigenes alike, before independence: Peter Sack, for example, was fearful of deforestation, soil erosion, overgrown mines, run-down plantations, towns strangled by parasitic squatter settlements, a handful of glamorous tourist resorts, murder and mayhem on the highways, and corrupt politicians jetting abroad at every opportunity.[82] There was fire enough in 1974 to justify all this smoke; and there still is. But the most pessimistic forecasts have not been borne out. The pace of development has been rapid – but it has been confined in the main to a few urban centres, and still fewer hives of industry such as Bougainville. Villagers have neither had the time nor the inclination to commit themselves to the town: indeed, many urban workers return 'home' after a spell in town, much as plantation labourers did before the war. In many areas of PNG, as Vulliamy says, 'there is a strong allegiance to traditional village culture, which facilitates the potential return of school leavers'.[83]

Sack called his book The Problem of Choice. Where education, at least, is concerned, the choice has still to be made. The alternatives of compulsion and discretion; universality and selection; the formal schooling of children and the non-formal education of adults; classroom teaching and village-based learning; the adoption of international examining methods and the local assessment of capability – all these alternatives (and many others) are still wide open. Education is already institutionalised – it is recognisably a *system* – but it is not yet fossilised. It was not too late, in the 1970s, for government ministers to propose and debate the abolition of the national high schools and of university grants, mother-tongue teaching, the economic self-sufficiency of schools, the encouragement of private foundations (the Education Minister, Mr Oscar Tammur, was himself the proprietor of a private high school), and much else equally radical and exploratory. There was argument from first principles, not entrenched positions. There was an open-mindedness at all levels, and a preparedness to listen to non-establishment views. Secretary of Education Alkan Tololo could question the western model of education in these unselfconscious terms:

It served a need – an introduced need. Whether it continues to serve the needs of the countries in which it was introduced is a different matter.

Papua New Guineans themselves must decide what, for them, is the 'good life'. Then it is possible to consider alternative ways of reaching their goals.[84]

Western education had not delivered the goods that had been promised. It had been one more road leading to yet one more road, in what looked increasingly like an immense maze. The white man had led the native in, in quest of the cargo at the end. Now that the native has learned that there is no end, there is no one but himself to lead him out again.

References

[1]Worsley (1970), p. 277.

[2]Stent (1977), p. 217.

[3]Downs (1972), pp. 64, 65.

[4]'Cash crops or cargo?' by T. G. Harding and P. Lawrence, in Epstein *et al.* (1971), p. 213.

[5]Seifert (1976), p. 87.

[6]Lawrence, *'The Ngaing of the Rai Coast'*, in Harding and Wallace (1970), p. 303.

[7]Todd (1974), p. 51.

[8]Morauta (1974), p. 51.

[9]Conton, William, *The African*, London, Collins (1959), p. 20.

[10]Ashton (1977), p. 140.

[11]McNamara, V., 'High school selection and the breakdown of village society', 1971, in Thomas (1976), p. 71.

[12]Weeks (1976), p. 147.

[13]McDonald, Ian, *The Humming-Bird Tree*, London, HEB (1974).

[14]Kavani, Siump, 'The drop-out' in Beier (1974), p. 62.

[15]Giraure, Nelson, *The need for a cultural programme* in Brammall & May (1975), p. 104; and Thomas (1976), p. 63.

[16]Frankel (1976), p. 121.

[17]'Educate daughters', *Port Moresby Post-Courier*, 23 August 1978.

[18]Olewale, Ebia, 'The impact of the University on village communities' in Thomas (1976), p. 124.

[19]Frankel (1976), p. 129.

[20]Vambe, Lawrence, *An Ill-Fated People*, London, HEB (1972), p. 236.

[21]Fry, N. H., 'Population growth and education planning' in New Guinea Research Unit (1970), p. 82.

[22]Welsh (1976), p. 3.

[23]Clarke (1975), p. 392.

[24]Hogbin (1951), p. 188.

[25]Kambipi, T. M., 'Cash-cropping and population pressure' in Sack (1974), p. 127.

[26]Seifert (1976), p. 83.

[27]Mwangi, Meja, *Kill me Quick*, London, HEB (1973), p. 1.

[28]Keating, D. A., 'Form 2 School-leavers and Brandi high school' in Weeks (1976), p. 208.

[29]Conroy, John, 'Dilemmas of educational policy' in Clunies-Ross and Langmore (1973), p. 160.

[30]Strathern, Marilyn, 'The disconcerting tie: attitudes of Hagen migrants towards home' in May (1977), p. 260.

[31]Rowley (1965), p. 207.

[32]Ryan, Dawn, 'Toaripi in Port Moresby and Lae' in May (1977), p. 150.

[33]Koroma, Joseph, 'A Study of the Bundi people in urban Goroka' in ibid., p. 212.

[34]Gunton, R. J., 'A banker's gamble' in Sack (1974), p. 112.

[35]'Thieves come to steal and bash', *Port Moresby Post-Courier*, 10 March 1978.

[36]Conroy in Clunies-Ross and Langmore (1973), p. 149; and Fry in New Guinean Research Unit (1970), p. 81.

[37]'Class Society is the cause', *Port Moresby Post-Courier*, 20 March 1978.

[38]Clarke (1975), p. 339.

[39]Eri (1973), p. 45.

[40]Hogbin (1951), p. 190.

[41]Seifert (1976), p. 86.

[42]McGregor (1976), p. 190.

[43]Stent (1977), p. 196.

[44]Patrick, Bro., 'What is happening at St Xavier's' in Weeks (1976), p. 84.

[45]Wilson (1976), pp. 43–6.

[46]'Cargo cult threats to teachers' in Weeks (1976), pp. 35, 36.

[47]Foster, Philip, 'Dilemmas of educational development: what we might learn from the past' in Brammall and May (1975), p. 22.

[48]Welsh (1976), p. 2.

[49]'Eighty-six per cent enrolment target', *Port Moresby Post-Courier*, 5 December 1977.

[50]Silachot, E. and Kemelfield, G., 'Community secondary education project' in Department of Education (1979), p. 20.

[51]ibid., p. 22.

[53]'School fees revolt warned', *Port Moresby Post-Courier*, 31 January 1979.

[53]Young (1977), p. 21.

[54]Weeks (1978), p. 176.

[55]Odaga, Asenath, *The Villager's Son*, London, HEB (1971), p. 2.

[56]'Education '81', *Port Moresby Post-Courier*, 1 September 1981.

[57]Lancy (1979), p. 98.

[58]'Don't blame national teachers, they need to be taught', *Port Moresby Post-Courier*, 12 July 1978.

[59]Wilson (1976), p. 49.

[60]'A longitudinal study of school leaver migration', J. D. Conroy in May (1977), p. 115; 'The Hula in Port Moresby', N. D. Oram, in ibid., p. 146; 'School leavers in the villages', Michael Wilson, in Powell and Wilson (1974), p. 147; Weeks (1978), pp. 10, 35.

[61]Thomas (1976), p. 235.

[62]in Weeks (1978), p. 80.

[63]Feacham (1973), p. 37.

[64]Fisk, E. K. and Tait, Maree, 'Aid' in Hudson (1975), p. 107.

[65]Oram (1976), p. 225.

[66]Standish, W. A., 'Politics and societal trauma' in Sack (1974), p. 157.

[67]Welsh (1976), p. 4.

[68]Silvey (1978), p. 19.

[69]Conroy (1979), p. 2.

[70]Aluko, T. M., *Chief the Honourable Minister*, London, HEB (1970), pp. 133, 134.

[71]Sheehan, Barry A., 'The Vanishing School' in Thomas (1976), p. 87.

[72]Clarke (1975), p. 19.

[73]Lancy (1979), p. 100.

[74]Conroy (1979), p. 39.

[75]'Three more in Schools Project', *Port Moresby Post-Courier*, 28 May 1979.

[76]Stanton, Ron, 'Secondary schools community extension project: an innovation in high school education' in Department of Education (1979), p. 29.

[77]Vulliamy (1980), p. 60.

[78]ibid., p. 22.

[79]ibid.

[80]Vulliamy (1983), p. 22.

[81]ibid., p. 23.

[82]Sack (1974), p. 6.

[83]Vulliamy (1983), p. 3.

[84]Tololo, Alkan, 'A consideration of some likely future trends in education in PNG' in Brammall and May (1975), p. 5.

Conclusion

Since its first manifestation in Melanesia, cargoism has grown in sophistication. The early fascination by ritual – by singing, by prayer, and baptism – became awe of the 'Book'. Access to this was seen to be by means of literacy in English. Schooling, therefore, in part supplemented, and in part supplanted religious observance as the road to the cargo. A desire for primary education gave way to a desire for secondary education, and so for higher education, and all the diplomas and the prestige that this level conferred. Alongside the popular demand for education there grew a hunger – at least among urban graduates, and among coastal and island communities first in contact with Europeans – for self-government. Flag-raising, voting, sitting in the House of Assembly and passing bills came to be seen as the most potent of all rites of passage from subservience to self-sufficiency. It was the road to the cargo that other dependent nations had taken.

None of the ways led where it was hoped it would lead. None delivered the goods in the simplistic way so many Papua New Guineans hoped it would – even quite highly-educated Papua New Guineans. At each failure frustration mounted, and a 'new' way was sought. Of course, not all disaffected Papua New Guineans have turned to drink, or tobacco, or cards, or crime; or been beguiled by 'false prophets' into believing that if only they will invest in trucks and trade stores (or dig for coins in the river-bank) they will strike it rich. There has been much real economic development. Coffee estates have brought prosperity to the Eastern Highlands; copper has transformed Bougainville; cattle, pigs and poultry projects abound, and the annual Highland Show is attracting increasing numbers of foreign tourists, happy to exchange dollars and yen for a sight of the Stone Age. Where there has been economic development, cargoism has been quiescent. The means of achieving wealth (if not parity with Europeans) has lain to hand; and it has been seized upon both locally and nationally. An elite of politicians, businessmen, civil servants, and industrialists has emerged, sophisticated enough to negotiate with multi-national companies, and the trading nations of South-East Asia and the South Pacific, in matters affecting fishing, timber-felling, oil-prospecting, and copper-mining. But it would be a bold spirit who would assert that cargoism is a spent force. It is still manifest in traditional forms in the Western Highlands, among the Enga, and in villages and urban slums elsewhere. And cargoism is not dead, as an underpinning philosophy, even on the university campuses, and in the House of Assembly. Cargo activities may be muted, they may even be eradicated, or be laughed out of court. But the intractable, hard core epistemology of cargoism survives – and it deserves to be taken seriously.

The promise of material wealth was a stimulus to cargo movements inasmuch as natives were unable to understand how wealth could be generated by other than ritual means; or inasmuch as they were frustrated in their efforts to bring about development by means of what was perceived to be an appropriate, 'European' form of economic activity. At the same time, when the promise looked as if it was being kept, and development did 'take off' in unlikely places, the cargoist impulse was stayed. We have seen that the question arises whether economic development has been too rapid, or not rapid enough. Papua New Guinea has been put through a crash course in development. Can what has been done, in any sense, be undone? Can the big hole be filled in, and Bougainville be restored to its former innocence? Can the bright lights be dimmed, and the beer be returned to the water whence much of it came? Such questions answer themselves. If further 'development' proves to be elusive, if non-development is unpalatable, undevelopment is unthinkable.

We shall not ask whether there has been too much or too little education; but it is not unreasonable to ask whether there has been too much or too little schooling. Education has been both a cargo

cult – a road to European gnosis – and an antidote against the
naïveté of cargoism. Papua New Guinea does not yet enjoy
universal, free primary education. It will not be compulsory, and it
is unlikely that it will be free of charge, until the mid-1990s at the
earliest. It is not, therefore, too late to unravel some of the
provision that has been made, and that is being made, if the answer
to the question above is that there has been too much schooling.
There are those who would argue that, since there are too few jobs
in the cash economy, in towns, for all the graduates of ten years'
schooling (never mind those eased out of the system after Grades 8
and 6), would-be pupils and their parents should not be teased into
believing that school will 'lead' anywhere but 'back to the village'.
If young people are to be advised to return home to cultivate coffee,
or tea, or pyrethrum; or live by subsistence farming, selling off
surpluses; or by handicrafts; or by singing and dancing for tourists,
there are those would would say that conventional schooling will
merely make for unreal expectations, and explosive frustration.
And they would be right. But the existing provision of schooling
can no more be unravelled than the existing pattern of economic
activity. De-schooling of an Illich sort is not (and should not be)
more realistic an option in PNG, than it is in Australia or Britain.

Whether or not children are schooled, they will not be suffered to
remain long in blissful ignorance of the world, fishing and farming
in traditional ways, and remaining in the stations to which they
have been called. If they do not go to the world, the world will go
to them.

Sir Paul Hasluck was Minister for External Territories for nearly
13 crucial years (1950–63). He wrote in 1976: 'I have often been
criticised for allegedly concentrating on primary schools and not
doing enough to provide secondary schools . . .'[1] One reason for
this was his unwillingness to create an 'élite'; Murray used this
word in a way that Sir Paul found quite offensive. But there were
other reasons for the policy. The most important was that the
decision had been made that education was to be in English, the
foundation for which had to be laid early on. The decision can be
faulted, but the policy implication is undeniable. Sir Paul was not
opposed to post-primary education; there could be no roof – no
apex in a university – without a foundation, and a string of
secondary courses; but circumstances delayed advance. He was up

against the determination of expatriates to send their children to school in Australia – and his own, laudable refusal to establish racially segregated schools. And more seriously, he discovered that as soon as young people could read and write and count, they were in demand both by private employers and by the administration. Primary schools delivered the goods; therefore, as far as the general public (black and white) was concerned, secondary schools could wait.

Finally, there was the lack of teachers to contend with, and a poor sort of public servant to do the contending. It is ironical that Hasluck should so often have been called a 'paternalist' by younger men[2] when – if we are to credit his memoirs – he was the pioneer, the 'chief urger'[3] of the country's political advancement. If all his policies for PNG had been given effect (by less passive officers than Messrs Groves and Cleland) there is no telling how much readier the country might have been on Independence Day.

It may well be that the SSCEP schools will serve as a model for a less academic, less formal, less disorienting pattern of education for all; the cost of laying on any sort of education for all school-age children will be enormous. But the social-political cost of a move to deschool Papua New Guinea, to restrict schooling to those who can afford it, or to those in towns too young or too numerous to be harnessed to useful economic activity, would be no less enormous.

Whether Papua New Guinea, and countries similarly placed, find newer models for schooling than those we introduced to them, depends on our developing new models for ourselves. Can we advice PNG to revert to a system of elementary education for all, and secondary education for a select few? We could do so only if we wished this sort of system on ourselves. Can we argue for no more than a 'vocational' education – a job-related education with an optimistically (or perhaps pessimistically) 'rural bias'? We could do this if we could foresee what the economic future holds, and if we could engineer this future. Are we confident seers, and engineers, in our own developed countries? On the contrary, we speak of uncoupling education and the labour market. We dream of an 'education for leisure' that takes human account of economic necessity.

Hogbin, in 1951, spoke of the veneer of sophistication on mission converts.[4] 'When giving their views in broad daylight,' he said, they 'usually speak of the old spirits with derision . . . When questioned during the night, however, they reluctantly admitted to a lingering suspicion that perhaps, after all, there may be spooks'. How many of us in the 'developed' nations are in a similar position? We may well persuade ourselves that we have outgrown fears of the dark; but are there not vestiges of cargoism in our longstanding faith in formal schooling? In his novel *Fragments*, the Ghanaian writer Ayi Kwei Armah puts himself in the position of a young man who has recently returned from America where he has had a college education.[5] He is a 'been-to', who might be thought to have acquired a taste for western 'goods' – but who has not. He considers how the 'been-to' is seen as a kind of ghost. He

> has chosen, been awarded, a certain kind of death. A beneficial death, since cargo follows his return. Not just cargo, but also importance, power, a radiating influence capable of touching . . . all those who in the first instance have suffered the special bereavement caused by the been-to's going away . . . The been-to is the ghost in person returned to live among men, a powerful ghost understood in the extent that he behaves like a powerful ghost, cargo and all . . . In many ways the been-to cum ghost is and has to be a transmission belt for cargo.
>
> Out there in ancestral territory, beyond the cemetery, the goods are available in abundance; no doubt about that in Melanesian cargo mythology. 'Kill the pigs, burn the crop, and wait with faith . . .'

Then Armah asks himself the question that is implicit in the present work, raised now explicitly: 'So how close are we to the Melanesian Islands? How close is everybody?' To judge by the dreams of sustained growth, fast cars, show houses, foreign holidays, labour-free kitchens, restaurant meals, special offers, and competition prizes by which we are beguiled in the developed countries, we are all very close.

It would be reasonable to hope that cargo cultism, in its raw religious form, will give way to more realistic expectations. It cannot fairly be said to have done any harm – it has certainly done no more harm than any other communal expression of religious hope. But if cargoism is replaced by a less millenarian creed, the replacement must do something to explain, and mitigate, the imbalance of wealth between the educated and the under-educated, the graduates and the 'push-outs', the employed and the landless unemployed. To the extent that it does not address this inequality, deep dissatisfactions will persist and be a breeding-ground for unreal hopes and (perfectly defensible) demands.

In the decade since independence, PNG has enjoyed a stability that everybody hoped for but not everybody expected. What Ian Downs forecast in his apocalyptic novel *The Stolen Land* has not happened. But if the connection between schooling, and jobs and Toyotas and houses of man-made materials is severed altogether, it may happen that education itself will be discounted. Its roots do not go so deep that it cannot easily be plucked out. 'Education-for-its-own-sake' is an idea that has some meaning for Kilibob. If he did not still seek 'paua' and the 'rot bilong kago' for *their* own sakes, he would be better placed to preach simplicity to his brother Manup. In the short term he must deliver more of the goods that he has promised – he must learn to share the cargo. We cannot take stability for granted in the long term if he does not.

References

[1] Hasluck (1976), p. 87.
[2] ibid., p. 196.
[3] ibid., p. 169.
[4] Hogbin (1951), p. 267.
[5] Ayi Kwei Armah, *Fragments*, London, HEB (1974), pp. 228, 229.

Bibliography

Agard, John (1978), 'Deschooling PNG: Nonformal education for rural development in PNG', in *Catalyst* Vol. 8, No. 1, Goroka, Melanesian Institute for Pastoral & Social Economic Service (MIPSES)

Ashton, Jeremy (1977), 'Some thoughts on community education in PNG' in *Catalyst*, Vol. 7, No. 2, Goroka, MIPSES

Barrington, J. M. (1976), 'The accountability concept in development education' in *PNG Journal of Education*, Vol. 12, No. 2, Konedobu, PNG

Beier, Ulli (ed.) (1972), *The Night Warrior & Other Stories from PNG*, Milton, Queensland, The Jacaranda Press Pty

Beier, Ulli (ed.) (1974), *Niugini Lives*, Port Moresby, The Jacaranda Press Pty

Brammall, J. & May, Ronald J. (eds) (1975), *Education in Melanesia: Eighth Waigani Seminar*, Canberra, Research School of Pacific Studies, ANU Press

Brown, Paula (1973), *The Chimbu: A Study of Change in the New Guinea Highlands*, London, Routledge & Kegan Paul

Burridge, Kenelm (1960), *Mambu: A Melanesian Milennium*, London, Methuen

Burridge, Kenelm (1969), *New Heaven New Earth*, Oxford, Basil Blackwell

Chatterton, Percy (1974), *Day That I Have Loved*, Sydney, Pacific Publications

Clarke, Arthur (1975), *Education, Economy, & Society in PNG*, University of Nottingham, unpublished MPhil thesis

Clunies-Ross, Anthony, & Langmore, John (eds) (1973), *Alternative Strategies for PNG*, Melbourne, OUP

Conroy, J. D. (1972), 'Motives for post-primary school attendance' in *PNG Journal of Education*, Vol. 8, No. 3, Konedobu, PNG

Conroy, J. D. (ed.) (1979), *National Education Strategy: PNG Education Plan Review & Proposals*, Port Moresby, Institute of Applied Social & Economic Research (IASER)

Davies, David M. (1970), *Journey into the Stone Age*, London, The Travel Book Club

Department of Education (1978), *1977 Education Annual Report*, Port Moresby

Department of Education (1979), *Sixth Regional Consultation Meeting on the Asian Programme of Educational Innovation for Development* (Bangalore), Port Moresby

Downs, Ian (1972), *The Stolen Land*, Melbourne, The Wren Publishing Pty

Epstein, A. L. (1969), *Matupit: Land Politics, & Change among the Tolai of New Britain*, Canberra, ANU Press

Epstein, A. L., Parder, R. S. & Reay, Marie (eds) (1971), *The Politics of Independence: PNG 1968*, Canberra, ANU Press

Eri, Vincent (1973), *The Crocodile*, Port Moresby, Robert Brown & Associates/Penguin Books

Essai, Brian (1961), *Papua New Guinea: A Contemporary Survey*, Melbourne, OUP

Feacham, Richard (1973), 'The Christians & the Enga', in *New Guinea*, April 1973

Finney, Ben R. (1973), *Big Men & Business: Entrepreneurship & Economic Growth in the New Guinea Highlands*, Canberra, ANU Press

Fisk, E. K. (ed.) (1968), *New Guinea on the Threshold: Aspects of Social, Political, & Economic Development*, Canberra, ANU Press

Frankel, Stephen (1976), 'Mass hysteria in the New Guinea highlands', in *Oceania* Vol. 47, No. 2, University of Sydney

Fry, N. H. (1970), 'Population growth & educational planning', in *People & Planning in Papua and New Guinea*, Canberra, New Guinea Research Unit, ANU

Glasse, R. M. & Meggitt, M. J. (eds) (1969), *Pigs, Pearlshells & Women: Marriage in the New Guinea Highlands*, Englewood Cliffs, N.J., Prentice-Hall Inc.

Greicus, Mike (ed.) (1976), *Three Short Novels from PNG*, Auckland, Longman Paul Ltd.

Hallpike, C. R. (1977), *Bloodshed & Vengeance in the Papuan Mountains: The Generation Of Conflict in Tauade Society*, Oxford, OUP

Harding, Thomas G. & Wallace, Ben J. (eds) (1970), *Cultures of the Pacific: Selected Readings*, N.Y., Free Press/London, Collier-Macmillan

Hasluck, Paul (1976), *A Time for Building*, Melbourne University Press

Hastings, Peter (1973), *New Guinea: Problems & Prospects* (2nd edn.) Melbourne, Cheshire Publishing Pty Ltd.

Hogbin, H. Ian (1951), *Transformation Scene: The Changing Culture of a New Guinea Village*, London, RKP

Hudson, W. J. (ed.) (1975), *Australia's New Guinea Question*, Melbourne, Nelson

Jinks, B., Biskup, P. & Nelson, H. (eds) (1973), *Readings in New Guinea History*, Sydney, Angus & Robertson Pty Ltd.

Kiki, Albert Maori (1968), *Kiki: Ten Thousand Years in a Lifetime*, Melbourne, Cheshire Publishing Pty Ltd.

Lancy, David F. (1979), *Education Research 1976–9: Reports & Essays*, Port Moresby, Ministry of Education Science & Culture

Lanternari, Vittorio (1965), *The Religions of the Oppressed*, N.Y., New American Library

Lawrence, Peter (1964), *Road Belong Cargo*, Manchester University Press

Louisson, B. H. (1974), *Education Old & New in PNG*, Goroka, University Bookshop, UPNG

McCarthy, J. K. (1963), *Patrol into Yesterday: My New Guinea Years*, Melbourne, Cheshire Publishing Pty Ltd.

McGregor, Don (1976), 'Basic PNG assumptions' in *Catalyst*, Vol. 6, No. 3, Goroka, MIPSES

Malinowski, Bronislaw (1974), 'Baloma: The spirits of the dead in the Trobriand Islands' in *Magic, Science & Religion & Other Essays*, London, Souvenir Press

Matane, Paulias (1972), *My Childhood in New Guinea*, London, OUP

Matane, Paulias (1974), *Aimbe The Challenger*, Port Moresby, Niugini Press Pty Ltd.

May, R. J. (ed.) (1977), *Change & Movement: Readings on Internal Migration in PNG*, Canberra, ANU Press

Morauta, Louise (1974), *Beyond the Village: Local Politics in Madang, PNG*, Canberra, ANU Press

Nelson, Hank (1974), *Papua New Guinea: Black Unity or Black Chaos?*, Port Moresby, Robert Brown & Associates/Penguin Books

Oliver, Douglas (1973), *Bougainville: A Personal History*, Melbourne University Press

Oram, N. D. (1976), *Colonial Town to Melanesian City: Port Moresby 1884–1974*, Canberra, ANU Press

Palmer, Penny (1978), *Girls in High School in PNG: Problems of the Past, Present and Future*, Port Moresby, Education Research Unit, UPNG

Powell, J. P. & Wilson, M. (eds) (1974), *Education & Rural Development in the Highlands of PNG*, Port Moresby, UPNG

Read, Kenneth E. (1966), *The High Valley*, London, George Allan & Unwin

Roberts, A. M. (1977), 'Mathematics in provincial high schools 1976' in *PNG Journal of Education*, Vol. 13, No. 1

Rowley, C. D. (1965), *The New Guinea Villager: A Retrospect from 1964*, Melbourne, Cheshire Publishing Pty Ltd.

Ruhen, Olaf (1963), *Mountains in the Clouds*, Melbourne, Horwitz Publications Inc. Pty

Sack, Peter G. (ed.) (1974), *Problem of Choice: Land in PNG's Future*, Canberra, ANU Press/Port Moresby, Robert Brown & Associates

Seifert, William (1976), 'The man in the street: urbanisation as seen by the man in the street' in *Catalyst*, Vol. 6, No. 2, Goroka, MIPSES

Silvey, Jonathan (1978), *Academic Success in PNG High Schools*, Port Moresby, Education Research Unit, UPNG

Sinclair, James (1971), *The Highlanders*, Milton, Qld, The Jacaranda Press/Robert Brown & Associates

Smith, Geoffrey (1975), *Education in PNG*, Melbourne University Press

Smith Graham (1974), *Mendi Memories*, Melbourne, Thomas Nelson (Aus.) Ltd.

Smyth, W. John (1976), 'Economics education for living in a developing country' in *PNG Journal of Education*, Vol. 12, No. 1

Somare, Michael (1975), *Sana: An Autobiography of Michael Somare*, Port Moresby, Niugini Press

Souter, Gavin (1963), *New Guinea: The Last Unknown*, Sydney, Angus & Robertson Pty Ltd.

Steinbauer, Friedrich (1974), *Shaping the Future: PNG Personalities*, Madang, Kristen Press

Stent, W. R. (1977), 'An interpretation of a cargo cult' in *Oceania*, Vol. 47, No. 3, University of Sydney

Strathern, Andrew (1972), *One Father, One Blood: Descent & Group Structure Among the Melpa People*, London, Tavistock Publications

Strelan, John G. (1977), *Search for Salvation: Studies in the History & Theology of Cargo Cults*, Adelaide, Lutheran Publishing House

Thomas, E. Barrington (ed.) (1976), *Papua New Guinea Education*, Melbourne, OUP

Threlfall, Neville (1975), *One Hundred Years in the Islands: The Methodist/United Church in the New Guinea Islands Region 1875–1975*, Rabaul, Toksave Na Buk Dipatmen

Todd, Ian (1974), *Papua New Guinea: Moment of Truth*, Sydney, Angus & Robertson

Tomkins, Dorothea, & Hughes, Brian (1969), *The Road from Gona*, Sydney, Angus & Robertson

Trompf, Garry (1976), 'The theology of Big Wen' in *Catalyst*, Vol. 6, No. 3, Goroka, MIPSES

Trompf, Garry (ed.) (1977), *Problems of Melanesia: Six Essays*, Port Moresby, Institute of PNG Studies

University of Papua New Guinea (1976), *High School Leavers Look to their Future: A Study in Mendi & Tari*, Port Moresby, Education Research Unit, UPNG

Vulliamy, Graham (1980), *SSCEP & High School Outstations: A Case Study*, Port Moresby, Education Research Unit, UPNG

Vulliamy, Graham (1983), *The Secondary Schools Community Extension Project in PNG*, York, Department of Education, University of York, mimeo

Weeks, S. G. (ed.) (1976), *Education & Independence 1975, PNG: A Resource Book of Documents on Issues in Education*, Port Moresby, Education Research Unit, UPNG

Weeks, S. G. (ed.) (1977), *The Story of My Education: Autobiographies of*

Schooling in PNG, Port Moresby, Education Research Unit, UPNG

Weeks, S. G. (ed.) (1978), *Youth in their Villages*, Port Moresby, Education Research Unit, UPNG

Welsh, Thomas (1976), 'Community education & the 5-Year Plan' in *PNG Journal of Education*, Vol. 12, No. 2

White, Osmar (1965), *Parliament of a Thousand Tribes*, Melbourne, Wren Publishing Pty Ltd.

Willis, Ian (1974), *Lae: Village & City*, Melbourne, Melbourne University Press

Wilson, Michael (1976), 'School leavers in a coastal area' in *PNG Journal of Education*, Vol. 12, No. 1

Wolfers, Edward P. (1975), *Race Relations & Colonial Rule in PNG*, Brookvale, NSW, Australia & New Zealand Book Co.

Woolford, Don (1976), *Papua New Guinea: Initiation & Independence*, Brisbane, University of Queensland Press

Worsley, Peter (1970), *The Trumpet Shall Sound*, London, Granada Publishing Ltd.

Young, R. E. (1977), 'Education & the image of western knowledge in PNG' in *PNG Journal of Education*, Vol. 13, No. 1

Index